OSPREY AIRCRAFT OF THE ACES • 106

Spanish
Republican Aces

SERIES EDITOR: TONY HOLMES

OSPREY AIRCRAFT OF THE ACES • 106

Spanish Republican Aces

Rafael A Permuy López

OSPREY
PUBLISHING

Front Cover
Mark Postlethwaite's specially commissioned cover artwork captures the moment when the first two Italian Fiat CR.32s of the *Aviación del Tercio* were shot down over Talavera de la Reina, southwest of Madrid, on 31 August 1936. In the foreground, sargento piloto Andrés García La Calle, leading the fighter *patrulla* of capitán Juan Quintana y Ladrón de Guevara's *Escuadrilla Mixta*, based at Talavera, is at the controls of Hawker Spanish Fury '4-1'. He has just shot down the aircraft of Tenente Ernesto Monico, who can be seen taking to his parachute.

In the distance, two Hispano-Nieuport Ni-H.52s flown by cabos Roberto Alonso Santamaría and wingman Rafael Peña Dugo are shooting down the second CR.32 flown by Sergente Maggiore Castellani. The latter force-landed his Fiat fighter near Villanueva de la Serena and returned to friendly territory on foot. Monico, however, was captured by militants retreating towards Talavera. According to Republican sources he was subsequently shot dead while trying to escape, although this was refuted by the *Aviación del Tercio*, who claimed Monico was executed despite declaring his nationality and requesting to see the Italian ambassador in Madrid.

Once Tenente Monico's body was found, Fascist propaganda went mad, claiming that the slain aviator was a legendary 35-victory ace, when in reality he had never actually shot down an aircraft in combat. Tenente Monico was posthumously awarded Italy's highest military decoration, the *Medaglia d'Oro al valor Militare*.

The three Spanish pilots involved in this action later became aces, although Alonso would be killed in a flying accident while testing an I-15 *Chato* (Cover artwork by Mark Postlethwaite)

First published in Great Britain in 2012 by Osprey Publishing
Midland House, West Way, Botley, Oxford, OX2 0PH
44-02 23rd Street, Suite 219, Long Island City, NY, 11101, USA

E-mail; info@ospreypublishing.com

Osprey Publishing is part of the Osprey Group

A CIP catalogue record for this book is available from the British Library

ISBN: 978 1 84908 668 4
e-book ISBN: 978 1 84908 669 1
e-Pub ISBN: 978 1 78096 440 9

Edited by Tony Holmes and Bruce Hales-Dutton
Translated from Spanish by Juan Carlos Salgado
Page design by Tony Truscott
Cover Artwork by Mark Postlethwaite
Aircraft Profiles by Julio López Caeiro
Index by Alan Thatcher
Originated by PDQ Digital Media Solutions
Printed and bound in China through Bookbuilders

12 13 14 15 16   10 9 8 7 6 5 4 3 2 1

Osprey Publishing is supporting the Woodland Trust, the UK's leading woodland conservation charity by funding the dedication of trees.

www.ospreypublishing.com

ACKNOWLEDGEMENTS
The author wishes to express his gratitude to his friends Lucas Molina Franco and Canario Azaola Reyes for their selfless assistance in preparing this book. He also wants to thank Juan Conde and Francisco Queipo for scanning the photographs used in this volume. Finally, special thanks to Juan Carlos Salgado not only for his translation of the book's text into English but also for having incorporated corrections and important data into the manuscript. To them all, thank you very much.

CONTENTS

AUTHOR'S INTRODUCTION

O ver the years a number of books, magazine articles and websites have published lists of the Spanish Republican fighter pilots who became aces during the Civil War of 1936-39. It should be emphasised that all are unofficial and often contradictory. It should also be noted that they are based on their creator's personal interpretation, as there are no reliable official data sources to substantiate them from a historical perspective. The reader should also be aware that documents from official records in Spanish military archives regarding the *Fuerzas Aéreas* of the Spanish Republic rarely include data attributing aerial victories to individual fighter pilots.

There are two basic documents containing rigorous statistical studies of the performance of the Spanish Republican fighter force during the conflict. These are the daily *Partes de Operaciones* (Operational Reports) maintained by the 3ª *Sección (Operaciones)* of the staff of the government *Jefatura de las Fuerzas Aéreas* (Air Force Headquarters) and the *Diario de Operaciones de la Escuadra de Caza* Nº 11 (operational record books of the 11th Fighter Group). Both documents are incomplete, and they attribute specific data on aerial victories not to individual pilots but to the different *escuadrillas* (squadrons) or *grupos* (groups) as a whole, or to *Escuadra de Caza* Nº 11 itself without further reference.

The second document is incomplete, and covers two different periods. The first runs from 1 October 1937, when the *Escuadra de Caza* was officially established, to 23 June 1938, but with several gaps during this period. The second starts on 23 September 1938 and ends on 23 January 1939. There are, therefore, many missing documents, particularly those containing details of the most important air operations of the Aragon campaigns – the offensive on Valencia, the operations in Extremadura and the initial phase of the crucial battle of the Ebro in July, August and September 1938. Also missing is coverage of the final days of the campaign in Catalonia from late January through to early February 1939.

Furthermore, the daily *Partes de Operaciones* were written in widely different styles, with varying content that is sometimes confusing and highly non-specific. Indeed, the accuracy of the entries often depended on who was the *Oficial de Información* (intelligence officer) writing them at the time within the Staff of *Escuadra* Nº 11. This is why it is very difficult to get precise data that enables every officially confirmed aerial victory to be attributed to a particular Republican fighter pilot. As far as possible, the author has managed to determine, albeit in an admittedly incomplete way, the scores of these pilots at different periods of the war.

The criteria for the choice of pilot biographies that follow in this book also require explanation. First of all, the aviators featured are the most outstanding pilots of the early months of the civil war, whose actions over the Central, Aragon and Andalusia fronts were widely reported in the contemporary press. The author has also thought it important to highlight the biographies of the *Escuadra de Caza* Nº 11 commanding officers, the commanders of the I-16-equipped *Grupo* Nº 21 and the I-15-equipped *Grupo* Nº 26 and the most significant *escuadrilla* commanders of both groups. Last, but by no means least, the book details the exploits of notable pilots operating on the unique front of northern Spain, which included the Basque Country, Santander and Asturias. Here, Republican fighter pilots had to fight in difficult operational conditions against a numerically superior enemy. The activities of the most significant nightfighter pilots are detailed too.

The author hopes the reader will be able to accept his personal selection of Spanish government fighter pilots and forgive him for any particular gaps.

Rafael A Permuy López
Madrid, March 2012

REPUBLICAN FIGHTER FORCE IN 1936-37

At the beginning of the Spanish Civil War in July 1936, two of the three fighter groups of the *Aviación Militar* – *Grupo de Caza* Nº 11 (11th Fighter Group) based at Getafe, near Madrid, and *Grupo de Caza* Nº 13 at El Prat de Llobregat airfield, near Barcelona, remained in government-held territory. The third, *Grupo de Caza* Nº 12, based at Armilla, near Granada, had been disbanded a few days before the military uprising. One of its *escuadrillas* (squadrons), commanded by capitán (captain) José Méndez Iriarte, was posted to Madrid. The other unit, led by capitán Joaquín Pérez y Martínez de la Victoria, sent its aircraft to the *Parque Regional de Aviación* (depot) at Tablada airfield, near Seville.

Normal equipment of Spanish fighter units at this time was the Hispano-Nieuport Ni-H.52, built under licence by Hispano-Suiza at Guadalajara. About 60 of the 135 acquired remained in service in government-held areas. As for personnel, in Madrid those who supported the Republican government included *Grupo* Nº 11 CO, capitán Manuel Cascón Briega, and two capitanes *jefes de escuadrilla* (squadron commanders), Avertano González Fernández-Muñiz and José Méndez Iriarte. Other Republic supporters were teniente (lieutenant) Francisco Márquez Yanguas and suboficiales (NCOs) Antonio Andrés Pascual, Gonzalo García San Juan, Andrés García La Calle and Manuel Aguirre López and cabos (corporals) Jesús García Herguido, Roberto Alonso Santamaría and Rafael Peña Dugo. They were subsequently joined by tenientes Luis Iglesias Gracia and Ramón Puparelli Francia. Upon the outbreak of the conflict these pilots defended the vast central front, as well as the north of Spain, and they were soon reinforced by volunteer pilots and foreign mercenaries.

At *Grupo* Nº 13 in Barcelona the Nationalist uprising was opposed by capitán Francisco Ponce de León y Díaz de Velasco and oficiales subalternos Amador Silverio Jiménez and Adonis Rodríguez González, as well as by sargentos (sergeants) José Cabré Planas, Jesús García Herguido, Fernando Roig Villalta, Alfonso Jiménez Bruguet,

The Hispano-Nieuport Ni-H.52 was the standard fighter in the Spanish air force before the civil war. At the start of the conflict it equipped *Grupo de Caza* Nº 11, based at Madrid's Getafe airfield, as seen in this photograph, and *Grupo de Caza* Nº 13

Emilio Villaceballos García and Jaime Buyé Berni. These men, together with a Ni-H.52 *escuadrilla,* covered the Aragon. Three pilots, Ponce de León, Silverio and Villaceballos, were even deployed to airfields in the north, the latter two aviators flying Ni-H.52s to Bilbao to cover the Bay of Biscay front.

At Los Alcázares airfield at Mar Menor, where the *Escuela de Tiro y Bombardeo Aéreo* (Aerial Gunnery and Bombing School) was based, there was a Ni-H.52 flight available for gunnery practice. Its CO was teniente Aurelio Villimar Magdalena, and he was supported by teniente Antonio de Haro López and sargentos pilotos José Jiménez Resino, Augusto Martín Campos, Ángel López Pastor and cabo Rafael Robledano. These resources were sufficient to cover the eastern and central Andalusian fronts, and also to detach elements to the two airfields at Guadix, in Granada, and El Rompedizo, in Málaga.

As for the *Marina de Guerra* (Navy) air arm located at the *Base Aeronaval* (Naval Air Base) at San Javier and also at the Mar Menor, in Murcia, there was an *Escuadrilla de Combate y Acompañamiento* (Escort Fighter Squadron) equipped with Martinsyde F 4 Buzzard fighters. Although outdated, these aircraft – 20 of which had been supplied to Spain in the early 1920s – would be briefly used during the early days of the military uprising. This unit was led by oficial tercero (sub lieutenant) Carlos Lázaro Casajust, who commanded auxiliares (NCOs) Javier Jover Rovira, Herminio Moro Álvarez and Manuel Mora Deutú. Additional fighter pilots, although serving within army Ni-H.52 *escuadrillas,* subsequently joined the naval air arm. They were auxiliares Luis Alonso Vega, Carlos Colom Moliner, Tomás Baquedano Moreno, Eduardo Guaza Marín and Antonio Blanch Latorre.

—— EARLY REPUBLICAN FIGHTER FORCE ——

During the first phase of the civil war the government fighter force was poorly utilised, being dispersed in small flights of two or three aircraft only. Because of this policy equipment soon became worn out, resulting in serious losses that decimated the ranks of the Republican fighter pilots.

The arrival of 14 Dewoitine D.372 parasol-winged fighters in mid August 1936 and six gull-winged Loire Nieuport 46 C1s in September (mostly flown by British and French pilots) did nothing to balance the scales, particularly as they were strongly opposed by newly arrived Heinkel He 51 and Fiat CR.32 fighters. Most of the surviving government fighter pilots in Madrid soon fell in air combat or were moved to desk jobs. During the first phase of the conflict it was the most prominent tenientes and capitanes who were given command of the fighter units then being formed.

Grupo de Caza Nº 13, based at El Prat, in Barcelona, had only one Ni-H.52 *escuadrilla*. This unit remained loyal to the government. The *grupo* badge was a green four-leaf clover on a black disc, which was worn on the fin of each fighter

By that time the most distinguished fighter pilots on the central front were Andrés García La Calle, Roberto Alonso Santamaría, Rafael Peña Dugo, Manuel Aguirre López and Félix Urtubi Ercilla. Most prominent in Aragon were José Cabré Planas and Jesús García Herguido, while in the south it was Ángel López Pastor and Rafael Robledano Ruiz who excelled. Soon, two *escuadrilla* COs and at least four or five pilotos subalternos had been killed in air combat. Equipment attrition was such that by late October 1936 there was only one fighter available to defend the whole of the Madrid front.

Things began to change from early November 1936 with the arrival of Soviet-supplied Polikarpov I-15 and I-16 fighters, soon to be dubbed *Chatos* and *Moscas*, together with Soviet personnel. Soon Spanish pilots were beginning to be attached to Soviet fighter units to become familiar with the new equipment, but during the first few months of the Polikarpov fighters' employment in the civil war it was the Soviet pilots who bore the brunt of the fighting in the air (see *Osprey Aircraft of the Aces 95 – Polikarpov I-15, I-16 and I-153 Aces* for details on the exploits of Soviet and non-Spanish aces in the civil war).

It was not until February 1937 that the first Spanish I-15 *Chato* fighter *escuadrilla* was established under the command of capitán Andrés García La Calle. Shortly afterwards a second was formed under capitán Roberto Alonso Santamaría. Both were soon thrown into action, the former in the battle for the Jarama and the latter on the Aragon front. The units also took part in the battle of Guadalajara. The squadrons were commanded by capitán Ramón Puparelli Francia, who was the first CO of the short-lived *Grupo de Caza* Nº 16, which comprised both *escuadrillas*. Puparelli then moved to Aragon with Alonso Santamaría's *escuadrilla*, while García La Calle's remained on the Madrid front.

In May 1937 significant fighter reinforcements had to be sent to the threatened Northern front. Two I-15 *Chato* units were moved via France, one led by capitán Alfonso Jiménez Bruguet and the second commanded by capitán Javier Jover Rovira. In both cases the aircraft were stopped by the French authorities at Pau and Toulouse. Finally, two forces, commanded by tenientes pilotos Gerardo Gil Sánchez and José Riverola Grúas, managed to reach Santander and Bilbao from Madrid. In July 1937 capitán Ramón Puparelli took reinforcements to the north, this time including examples of the new I-16 *Mosca* monoplane flown by Soviet pilots. A last expedition, comprising nine Spanish-flown fighters, arrived in Santander on 17 August, by which time the enemy offensive in the northern province had already started.

The Polikarpov-equipped fighter units operating on the Central front remained under Soviet command during the operations at La Granja (Segovia), Huesca, Brunete and Belchite during the summer and autumn of 1937.

Roberto Alonso Santamaría

Roberto Alonso Santamaría was born in Saragossa on 31 January 1908. In 1929 he enrolled at the Farman flying school at Toussus-le-Noble, in France, where he gained his private pilot's licence in June of that year. Alonso Santamaría volunteered for the *Aviación Militar* six months later and was posted to Tablada airfield, Seville, with the rank of private.

Holding a pilot's licence enabled him to apply for the military flying course, and he subsequently gained his wings on 22 October 1930. In 1931 Alonso Santamaría was posted to the 4º *Batallón de Aviación* deployed in the Spanish Moroccan protectorate, where he joined an *escuadrilla* based at Larache airfield. On 14 November he was posted to *Grupo de Caza* Nº 13 of *Escuadra* Nº 3 in Barcelona.

On 30 January 1932 Alonso Santamaría was told to fly Ni-H.52 '3-6' from Getafe to Barcelona, but engine trouble resulted in him force-landing at Morata de Jalón, Saragossa. That year, too, he qualified as an air gunner-bombardier at Los Alcázares airfield, and he was promoted to the rank of corporal in October 1933. On 30 May 1935 Alonso Santamaría flew with his unit to Barajas airfield,

Adjunto tengo el honor de remitir a V.S.fotografia en duplicado eje plar perteneciente al Cabo Piloto de la 2ª Escuadrilla de este Grup ROBERTO ALONSO SANTAMARIA por si tiene a bien disponer lo convenie te para que le sea expedido titul de la citada especialidad y las (Mecanico y Ametrallador Bombarder Granada 20 de Diciembre de 1.9? El Jefe de Aeroaromo Acctal. Jose Mendez Iriarte.

This document (an application form for the issuing of a military pilot ID card) includes a photo of then cabo Roberto Alonso Santamaría

Madrid, where, on 2 June, he participated in an airshow watched by the president of the Republic. That same month he was posted to Armilla airfield, Granada, where he joined the 2ª *Escuadrilla* of the newly established *Grupo de Caza* Nº 12, which was part of *Escuadra de Aviación* Nº 2 (2nd Wing). In early July 1936 the *grupo* was disbanded, and cabo Alonso Santamaría moved to Getafe airfield with his *escuadrilla*, which was led by capitán Méndez Iriarte.

When the civil war started Alonso Santamaría was still at Getafe, having been assigned to *Grupo de Caza* Nº 11. He participated in early combat missions flying Ni-H.52s with cabo Rafael Peña Dugo as part of sargento Andrés García La Calle's fighter *patrulla* (flight). On 25 July 1936 he claimed his first victory, over a Breguet 19, which he

The Hawker Spanish Fury was intended to replace the obsolete Ni-H.52, but only three examples had been delivered to Spain from the UK by July 1936. They were supposed to be used as pattern aircraft by Hispano-Suiza for its licence production of the Spanish Fury in the company's Guadalajara factory

forced to land at Grajera airstrip. In August García La Calle's fighter *patrulla*, made up of a Hawker Spanish Fury and two Nieuport Ni-H.52s, moved to the Herrera del Duque and Don Benito airfields at Extremadura. Later in the month the unit was sent to Talavera de la Reina airfield, in Toledo, and on the 31st Alonso Santamaría, with his wingman Rafael Peña Dugo, managed to shoot down a CR.32. Both men were promoted to the rank of sergeant following their success. On another occasion the pair engaged a He 51 flown by Teniente Julio Salvador. Although they believed they had downed the Heinkel fighter, the enemy pilot managed to reach his airfield.

Promoted to alférez (second lieutenant) on 8 September 1936, Alonso Santamaría continued flying with García La Calle's *patrulla* at Getafe airfield. Because of the overwhelming number of enemy CR.32s in the area, government pilots refused to fly alone from the late summer of 1936. Although the *Jefatura de Aviación* (Air Force Staff) did not agree to their operating in groups, the pilots' indiscipline was not punished.

On 15 November 1936 Alonso Santamaría was promoted to teniente, and a short while later he joined the Soviet I-15 *escuadrilla* led by kapitan Ivan Ivanovich Kopets (pseudonym 'José') at Alcalá de Henares, in Madrid. Other pilots in the unit at this time included tenientes García La Calle, López Trinidad, Galera Macías, Cuartero Pozo, Guaza Marín, Roig Villalta, García Herguido, Jiménez Bruguet, Aguirre López and Robledano Ruiz. The squadron fought on the Madrid front.

Promoted to capitán on 1 February 1937, Alonso Santamaría next commanded a new I-15 *escuadrilla*, which was established at Los Alcázares and San Javier. From there he moved to El Soto airfield, again on the Madrid front, and a new *escuadrilla* comprising tenientes Rafael Robledano Ruiz, Juan Comas Borrás, Antonio Blanch Latorre, Ricardo Rubio Gómez, Mariano Palacios Menéndez, Ángel Álvarez Pacheco, Justo García Esteban and Hipólito Barbeito Ramos, sargentos Manuel García Gascón, Alfonso Calvo Ortiz, Cándido Palomar Agraz and Rafael Magriñá Vidal and Uruguayan teniente Luis Tuya.

Following enemy air raids on the power stations in Catalonia, the *Jefatura de Operaciones* (Operations Command) of the *Fuerzas Aéreas* ordered capitán Alonso Santamaría's I-15-equipped 2ª *Escuadrilla* to the airfield at Lérida on 20 February. The eight-strong I-15 *escuadrilla* moved

Alonso Santamaría scored his first victories flying *Grupo* Nº 11 Ni-H.52s. Note the red band around the fuselage and the unit's black panther emblem on the fin. One of the government's Spanish Furies can also be seen in the background

to Lérida the following day, with capitán Ramón Puparelli leading the Spanish *Grupo de Caza*. Its mission was a simple one – protect the Tremp and Camarasa power stations. In March 1937 capitán Alonso Santamaría moved to Alcalá de Henares airfield with two patrols, the third remaining on the Aragon front to participate in Guadalajara operations.

The following month the unit returned to the Aragon front, where Alonso Santamaría and his *escuadrilla* were involved in the various aerial clashes that took place in this area during April. Tuya and Calvo were shot down, but the Republican pilots in turn claimed to have destroyed seven He 51s, although the enemy only admitted the loss of two aircraft.

Alonso Santamaría was finally withdrawn from frontline flying in the late spring of 1937, whereupon he test flew newly built I-15s emerging from the SAF-3 aircraft factory at Reus, in Tarragona. Having survived many months of combat, he was killed when his *Chato* caught fire and crashed during a test flight from Sabadell, in Barcelona. The date of Alonso Santamaría's demise remains unknown. He was a close friend of ace García La Calle, being romantically involved with one of his sisters.

Fernando Romero Tejero

Fernando Romero Tejero was born in Alcázar de San Juan, Ciudad Real, on 2 January 1904. He joined the *Arma de Aviación* (Aviation Corps) in July 1924 as a student mechanic at the *Escuela* at Cuatro Vientos, in Madrid. Tejero graduated in May 1925 and was posted to *Escuadrilla* AME VI, named after the aircraft it operated. In June 1926 he transferred to a Loring R-I reconnaissance *Escuadrilla* based at Tetuán and Larache airfields, in Morocco. In February 1927 the unit returned to Cuatro Vientos, and in September of the following year Tejero was accepted into the *Escuela Civil* (Civilian Flying School) at Albacete. Promoted to cabo in December 1928, he subsequently graduated as a piloto militar in March 1929 and was posted to León airfield.

Three months later Tejero had his first experience of flying a fighter when he was posted to the *Escuadrilla Martinsyde* of the *Grupo de Instrucción* (Training Group) at Getafe. He took part in an air-sea training exercise in the Mediterranean during this period. Then, in March 1930, came another posting, this time to *Escuadrilla* Breguet 19 of the same *grupo*, where he was promoted to sargento piloto in April. In 1931 Tejero returned to fighters, this time Ni-H.52s built locally at Getafe and issued to newly established *Grupo* Nº 13 based at El Prat de Llobregat. The following year he took an aerial gunnery and bombardier's course at Los Alcázares airfield, from which he graduated on 20 July. In August Tejero was posted to *Escuadra* Nº 2 in Seville, joining *Grupo* Nº 22 equipped with Loring R-III reconnaissance aircraft. That

The *Socorro Rojo Internacional* (International Red Relief) ID card of pilot Fernando Romero Tejero. He was a member of the Spanish Communist Party

October he applied for a new posting, to the *Escuadrilla* Y-2 at the *Escuela de Tiro y Bombardeo* at Los Alcázares, where he served until 1936.

At the start of the civil war sargento Romero Tejero joined the Nieuport fighter *patrulla*, established within *Escuadrilla* Y-2 at Los Alcázares. Teniente Aurelio Villimar assumed command of the unit and Romero played an active role in the capture of the seaplane base at La Ribera, in Murcia. Villimar was subsequently relieved by teniente Alarcón, who, on 27 July, flew Ni-H.52 '3-87' to Guadix, accompanied by Romero Tejero in '3-24'. Alarcón crashed on landing, suffering slight leg injuries. When replacement aircraft '3-42', flown by sargento Ángel López Pastor, arrived overhead Guadix, it was attacked in error by Romero Tejero! Fortunately, López Pastor escaped unscathed.

The following day Romero Tejero flew Ni-H.52 '3-24' to Andújar airfield, in Jaén, to escort two Breguet 19s. While based there he took off to intercept enemy aircraft, but engine failure caused him to force-land. Emerging from his wrecked fighter with both leg and eye injuries, Romero Tejero was admitted to hospital at Andújar and subsequently sent back to Los Alcázares on 30 July. Although he had not fully recovered, Romero Tejero was allowed to return to his *escuadrilla*. By 11 August he was again flying a Ni-H.52 from Guadix, and on the 13th he shot down two Nationalist Breguet 19s. The first crashed at Venta Navas and the second at Pinos Puente. Upon returning home, Romero Tejero was congratulated by both the local committee and the CO of Los Alcázares airfield, comandante (Maj) Ortiz, who was making a tour of inspection at the time.

Romero Tejero continued flying Ni-H.52s and was involved in several combats during this period, including one with a CR.32 in the Iznalloz area of Granada. He also undertook numerous patrol and reconnaissance sorties from Albacete, Valencia and Los Alcázares, as well as hazardous night flying. Although he lacked nocturnal flying experience, Romero Tejero took off on his own initiative to intercept enemy raiders on the night of 19/20 October He engaged a Nationalist tri-motor (probably a Ju 52/3m) and watched it explode over the sea ten miles west of Cartagena naval base. The claim was officially confirmed by comandante

Romero Tejero was detached at Guadix airfield, in Granada, when he first saw combat with Nationalist aircraft

Ortiz. The following month Romero Tejero was promoted to teniente, having logged 80 sorties and 65 flying hours in Ni-H.52 fighters.

Having not fully recovered from his wounds after his crash landing on 30 July, teniente Romero Tejero was withdrawn from frontline duties and posted to the *Escuadrilla de Transportes* (Transport Squadron), operating between Los Alcázares and Madrid. It was while flying one of its liaison aircraft on 29 December 1936 that he was involved in yet another flying accident.

In early 1937 Romero Tejero was appointed secretary to the CO of Los Alcázares airfield and put in charge of the *Oficina de Información y Cartografía* (Intelligence and Mapping Office). On 3 October 1938 he was appointed CO of the 6º *Sector Aéreo* (Air Area Nº 6) at Hellín, in Albacete. In February 1939 Romero Tejero became CO of the 3º *Sector Aéreo* at Los Llanos, again in Albacete. Promoted to capitán on 1 September 1938, Romero Tejero had the sad job of surrendering the airfield to Nationalist command at war's end. He was subsequently court-martialled and sentenced to 20 years imprisonment. No further data is available on him.

Felix Urtubi Ercilla

Born in Vitoria, Álava Félix Urtubi Ercilla joined the *Arma de Aviación Militar* as a student mechanic at the *Escuela de Mecánicos de Aviación Militar* (Air Force Mechanics' School) at Cuatro Vientos, from which he graduated in February 1927. As a *soldado mecánico* he enrolled in a flying course and graduated in November 1929. Ercilla was promoted to sargento in January 1934, and on the 23rd of that month he was posted to *Escuadra* Nº 1 at Getafe. On 28 April 1936 Ercilla was transferred to the *Fuerzas Aéreas de África* (African Air Forces), and he flew his first sorties with the 1ª *Escuadrilla* of Breguet 19-equipped *Grupo* Nº 1 from Tetuán airfield.

When the military uprising started in July 1936, sargento Ercilla began flying sorties over the Straits of Gibraltar with the Nationalists. However, a few days later he devised a plan to join the forces loyal to the government. So it was that on 25 July a Breguet 19 heading from enemy territory landed at Getafe airfield. Coded '1-12', the aircraft belonged to 1ª *Escuadrilla* of *Grupo* Nº 1 of the *Fuerzas Aéreas de África*, based at Tetuán. Sargento Félix Urtubi Ercilla had flown it across half the Iberian peninsula. The aircraft was also carrying the body of teniente Juan Miguel de Castro Gutiérrez, an Observador de Aeroplano (Aviation Observer) from *Grupo de Regulares* Nº 1 (Colonial Troops) based at Ceuta and Melilla. Félix Urtubi told journalists in Madrid;

'We left Tetuán at 0600 hrs today. We were ordered to strafe and bomb the government column travelling from La Línea. There were three aircraft. At an altitude of 1000 ft over the Straits of Gibraltar I turned to the teniente and shot him four times – in the forehead, in the chest and through the mouth. I didn't give the traitor time to look at me in dismay and cry "No! No!"

'Under the circumstances I was ready to flee to Valencia or Barcelona, cities which, according to the reports available in Morocco, had remained loyal to the Republic. I was ready to jump into the sea if the teniente was only wounded and reacted, but, as I suspected, he was dead. I flew into the darkness and made for here. I was ready to do anything. I'd rather die than surrender to the traitors to the government.

'With very little fuel left I landed at Getafe, and when the officers pointed their guns at me, I put mine to my temple and asked if Madrid was in Republican hands? If not I'd have shot myself rather than surrender. The officers were so moved they embraced me. Then I handed over the corpse of the teniente, whose name I don't know. He wasn't carrying any documents.'

A studio portrait of sargento piloto Félix Urtubi Ercilla, the first 'official hero' of the Republican fighter force

Urtubi's Hawker Spanish Fury '4-2' was captured intact by the Nationalists at Alburquerque, in Badajoz, after a forced landing caused by a faulty propeller. The pilot managed to escape back to Republican-held territory and '4-2' was repaired and issued to a Nationalist fighter unit

This account is confirmed by sargento piloto García La Calle. When Urtubi saw capitán Antonio Urzáiz Guzmán – reputed to be a monarchist – on the tarmac at Getafe he thought that Madrid was in rebel hands. Although Urzáiz had indeed taught King Alfonso XIII's children, he was a staunch defender of the Republican regime.

Urtubi was promoted to the rank of alférez and posted to *Grupo de Caza* Nº 11, and by mid-August 1936 he had been detached with Hawker Spanish Fury '4-2' to Don Benito airfield. While pursuing an enemy aircraft, the propeller of his own machine failed and Urtubi was forced to land near Alburquerque, a village in Nationalist-held Extremadura. He left his aircraft intact and made for friendly lines, which he reached disguised as a peasant holding the halter of a donkey. Once back at Getafe Urtubi was assigned a D.372, which he later turned over while landing at Santa Cruz de Mudela airfield, in Ciudad Real. He was given a Ni-H.52 upon his return to Getafe.

On 13 September a *patrulla* of *Aeronáutica Naval* Vickers Vildebeests arrived from Los Alcázares to reinforce the surviving Breguet 19s of *Grupo* Nº 31. Heading for the Talavera de la Reina front, and escorted by two Ni-H.52s flown by teniente Félix Urtubi Ercilla and auxiliar naval Carlos Colom Moliner, the Vildebeests were intercepted by three CR.32s led by future ranking Nationalist ace Capitán García Morato. The slow bombers managed to escape, but sergente Gianlino Baschirotto shot down Urtubi's Nieuport, which crashed in enemy territory. The CR.32 of Sergente Vincenzo Patriarca and the Ni-H.52 of auxiliar Colom collided in the heat of battle and both fighters crashed in government-held territory. The Italian-American pilot managed to bail out, despite having been wounded, and he was quickly taken prisoner when he landed. Colom, however, was killed, and the charred remains of his body were recovered and identified by his squadronmates.

Legend soon had it that it was Félix Urtubi who collided with the aircraft flown by Patriarca. Following the release of a brief communiqué, government war correspondents asked for the name of the airman involved to be released so that 'all the Spanish people can engrave it on their hearts'.

The following day Republican newspapers named teniente Félix Urtubi, and they attempted to give more details of the combat that had

Urtubi also flew Dewoitine D.372s, crashing one during a sortie from Santa Cruz de Mudela. A hastily camouflaged DC-2 can be seen in the hangar behind the French parasol fighter

ended in his death. *El Noroeste* contained a reasonably accurate version of events;

'Five enemy aircraft – two tri-motors and three fighters – were sighted over the Navalmoral road, but the tri-motors quickly turned tail in the presence of a loyal fighter pilot, who opened intense machine gun fire. He hit one of the tri-motors and then, when the latter vanished, began a hair-raising pursuit in the clouds, trying to hunt down the three enemy fighters. The loyal fighter pilot hit another enemy aeroplane, which also escaped, but he then pounced on a third enemy aeroplane and almost broke it in two. It was a dreadful clash. The enemy pilot parachuted from his aircraft. Our fighter also crashed. Our brave pilot succumbed to his injuries. Teniente Félix Urtubi is the name of our hero.'

But the dead Republican pilot was not Félix Urtubi. The remains were those of *Aeronáutica Naval* pilot Carlos Colom Moliner. This was made clear in the Madrid evening newspaper *La Voz* on 16 September. Under the heading 'Urtubi or Colom?' the paper reported;

'Today, we have been visited by two comrades from the *Aeronáutica Naval* who asked us to partially correct the information in the Madrid press on teniente Urtubi's alleged death. The corpse of the airman recovered from the Toledo field is that of auxiliar naval Carlos Colom. The fact that Urtubi was also flying at the same time over the same spot and on the same mission created all the confusion.

'Both airmen fought courageously, as we reported yesterday. It is thought that Carlos Colom succumbed when he attacked the enemy aeroplane with his aircraft. There is no news of Urtubi's whereabouts. We hope that he will be found safe. Whatever happens, Félix Urtubi and Carlos Colom have written a new and heroic page in the feats of loyal aviators.'

In fact, neither teniente Urtubi's Ni-H.52 nor his body were ever found in Republican territory. It is possible that his aircraft, shot down by sergente Baschirotto's CR.32, crashed in the rebel-held area. This is supported by the ministerial order promoting Félix Urtubi to capitán, which reported him as missing. Although Urtubi may have died a less glorious – but nonetheless tragic – death, this does nothing to denigrate his conduct during the uneven battle in which he lost his life.

Rafael Peña Dugo

Rafael Peña Dugo was born at Fuentecarreteros, in Córdoba, in 1906. Conscripted in 1927, he joined the *Aviación Militar* at the *Escuela de Mecánicos* at Cuatro Vientos, from which he graduated in February 1927. In August 1929 he was promoted to cabo mecánico and took a flying course the following year, graduating in October 1930. In January 1933 Peña qualified as an ametrallador bombardero (air gunner/bombardier) at the *Escuela de Tiro y Bombardeo* in Los Alcázares.

On 9 March 1932 Peña's Ni-H.52, coded '3-37', collided on take-off with '3-56' of cabo Máximo Ricote Juanas. Both pilots were unhurt, but their aircraft were seriously damaged. The accident was the subject of an inquiry, one result of which might have been Peña's failure to pass his examination for promotion to sargento in May of that year. Later in the civil war, however, Juanas became a capitán and commanded a Tupolev SB *Katiuska* bomber *escuadrilla*.

Upon the outbreak of war in Spain, Peña was posted as a cabo piloto to *Grupo de Caza* Nº 11, *Escuadra* Nº 1 at Getafe. Remaining loyal to the government and opposing the military uprising, his first sorties were flown over the Sierra in Madrid. He was impetuous and fired on friendly aircraft during the early days of the conflict, when both Republican and Nationalist air forces displayed similar markings on their machines. On one occasion Peña opened fire on a Republican Breguet 19, killing the observer, alférez Luis González Celma, and on 6 August 1936 he attacked friendly Ni-H.52s that had taken off from Barajas. Future ace Andrés García La Calle suffered a buttock wound, but *escuadrilla* CO, capitán José Méndez Iriarte, crashed in enemy-held territory and was killed.

On 31 August 1936 Peña was patrolling in a Ni-H.52 from Talavera de la Reina just as teniente coronel Yagüe's Nationalist columns were advancing on Madrid. The troops were supported by Italian-flown CR.32s, one of which Peña and squadronmate Roberto Alonso Santamaría managed to shoot down. Both pilots were promoted to alférez.

On 26 September 1936 a Nationalist Ju 52/3m flown by capitán Eustaquio Ruiz de Alda was shot down over Toledo and surviving crewmen murdered and their bodies mutilated. Some authors have attributed this victory to French pilot Jean Dary. According to Andrés García La Calle, alférez Rafael Peña Dugo, who had by now distinguished himself as a fine shot, downed the tri-motor. Everything seems to point to the conclusion that Dary, who also claimed two Ju 52/3ms in head-on attacks, was a member of the attacking Republican *patrulla*, however. The victory should, therefore, have been attributed jointly to the entire D.372 *patrulla*.

Luck deserted Rafael Peña the following day. During his second sortie six Republican fighters escorting a Potez 540 were attacked by five CR.32s led by future ace Capitán Ángel Salas, who chased the bomber. Sergente Manlio Vivarelli shot down the D.372 flown by alférez Rafael Peña, who bailed out with a leg wound. It is possible that British pilots Vincent Doherty and Eric Griffiths were also wounded during the same combat, although both managed to fly their D.372s back to Getafe airfield. Peña was initially treated at the hospital in Toledo, before being evacuated to Madrid just prior to the provincial capital falling into enemy hands. His wound eventually became gangrenous and his leg had to be amputated.

Peña was promoted to teniente and then capitán during his long period of convalescence in Alicante, where he remained until March 1937. Recovered from the worst of his wounds, and with a prosthetic leg, he was posted to France as inspector of one of the schools training Spanish Republican pilots. A letter mentioned in his personal records puts him in Paris on 31 October 1937. In January 1938 Peña was appointed Jefe de Estado

Rafael Peña also scored his first victories flying Ni-H.52s, before being assigned the Loire 46 parasol that is seen here providing the backdrop to this photograph. Peña was shot down over the Toledo front in the Loire, and he had to have a leg amputated due to the wounds he suffered in this incident

Mayor (Chief of Staff) of the *Agrupación de Defensa de Costas* (Coastal Defence Group). In March he became commander of Puigcerdá airfield and in May he was posted to the staff of *Grupo* Nº 71 of the *Fuerzas Aéreas*. Peña's service record notes that he logged 54 flying hours in June, July and August 1938, despite having only one leg. He was subsequently promoted to mayor (major).

At the end of the war Peña crossed the French border, and in January 1940 he was ordered to return to Spain, but went to the Soviet Union instead. Peña remained there during World War 2, although his handicapped condition barred him playing an active role in the conflict as an aviator. In the 1970s he was living in Dnepropetrovsk, and although no date of death is available, it seems likely Peña passed away in late 1980 or early 1981 – his death was reported in the *Boletín informativo* of the *Asociación de Aviadores de la República* issue No 13, January-February 1981.

Jesús García Herguido

Born at Velilla de Medinaceli, in Soria, on 18 January 1904, Jesús García Herguido started his working life as a mechanic-fitter with the La Mecánica company, before gaining employment in the MZA railway workshops at Alcázar de San Juan. He joined the *Escuela de Mecánicos* at Cuatro Vientos in July 1925 and graduated in October 1926. In 1928 Herguido was selected to join the crew of one of three Breguet 19s of *Grupo de Instrucción*, based at Getafe, for a special flight to Jerusalem. The *patrulla* took off on 28 May but the only aircraft to arrive in Palestine was that crewed by capitán Luis Roa and cabo mecánico García Herguido. They returned to Getafe on 11 June.

Herguido then attended a flying course at the *Escuela de Vuelo y Combate* (Combat Flying School) at Alcalá de Henares, from which he graduated in October 1930. Posted to *Grupo de Caza* Nº 13, based at El Prat de Llobregat, he was promoted to sargento piloto in December 1932. Herguido was still a member of this fighter unit when the civil war broke out in July 1936, although his initial combat sorties were bombing missions in Breguet 19s. The first of these was flown on 18 July, and two days later he targeted the rebel-held San Andrés Barracks in Barcelona.

On 2 August two Ni-H.52s flew from El Prat de Llobregat to the forward airfield at Sariñena, in Huesca, escorting four Breguet 19s during the flight. The Nieuports and their pilots, teniente Amador Silverio Jiménez and sargento Jesús García Herguido, remained at this location for some time. Fellow *Grupo* Nº 13 pilots sargentos Fernando Roig Villalta, José Cabré Planas, Jaime Buyé Berni and Emilio Villaceballos were flown to Sariñena in Breguet 19s, as was unit CO Alférez Alfonso Jiménez, and they all flew sorties in the Nieuports from the airfield. Jiménez' pilots, most of whom were officially still sargentos, were promoted to alférez by the Catalan *Generalitat* authorities, whose Consejero de Defensa (Secretary of Defence) was teniente coronel de Aviación Felipe Díaz Sandino. These promotions were officially confirmed on 31 August according to a decree dated 27 September.

The *Escuadrilla Mixta,* based at Sariñena, was unofficially called 'Alas Rojas' (Red Wings). This name was displayed on some of the unit's

Sargento García Herguido, nicknamed *'El Demonio Rojo'* ('The Red Devil'), poses alongside his Ni-H.52 at Sariñena airfield, in Huesca

vehicles, and it was also the title of the newspaper published at the Republican airfield.

The unit performed its first sortie on 3 August when Ni-H.52s escorted Breguet 19s sent to attack targets in the La Zaida area of the Aragon front. The following day the first aerial victory was recorded when Jesús García Herguido used his Nieuport fighter to shoot down a Nationalist Breguet 19 flown by capitán Eduardo Prado Castro, CO of an *escuadrilla* of *Grupo* Nº 23 detached to Saragossa. The aircraft made a forced-landing and both crewmen escaped unhurt. The resulting communiqué issued by the *Consejero de Defensa de la Generalitat* reported;

'Late this evening four Fascist aircraft from Andalusia tried to attack the advanced forces at La Zaida by taking advantage of today's stormy weather, which reduced visibility. A fighter aircraft of the Republic forces, flown by oficial señor Herguido, who was returning to base, engaged the four rebel aircraft and brought one down in flames. Aviator Herguido chased the other three beyond Saragossa, where he lost them. Returning to base, and over Saragossa, he noticed strong concentrations of rebel forces on the Paseo de la Independencia, which he strafed. Our airman returned safely to base.'

On 2 September, when Huesca was about to fall into Republican hands, the Nationalists hastily transferred two Ju 52/3m *escuadrillas* of the *Escuadra 'B'* and Comandante Juan Antonio Ansaldo's *Grupo 'Dragón'* to the Aragon front, where they flew several sorties against advancing Republican troops. Strangely enough, a government Ni-H.52 accompanied some of the Ju 52/3ms from their target to their airfield without attacking them. The fighter's Republican pilot may well have been alférez Jesús García Herguido, for that same day (date unknown) he had strafed the enemy airfield at Huesca, landed, saluted the astonished enemy airmen that ran up to his fighter with a tight fist and then taken off again! The prank was recorded in a communiqué from Barcelona, which noted 'The advance on Huesca goes on. A loyal aeroplane landed on the enemy airfield. It took off again safely'.

By then Herguido had acquired the nickname 'El Demonio Rojo' *('El Dimoni Roig'* in Catalan), and Republican war correspondents like Máximo Silvio praised him in the Catalan press. Regarded as one of the most courageous airmen operating over the Aragon front, he had racks for light 12 kg bombs fitted under the wings of his Ni-H.52. Thus equipped, Herguido dive-bombed enemy machine gun nests and harassed government forces marching on Huesca.

On 15 September there was further air combat in the Tardienta area involving Nieuport fighters from both sides. *Escuadrilla 'Alas Rojas"* Adonis Rodríguez González and alféreces Jesús García Herguido and Fernando Roig Villalta took off from Sariñena and headed for the front in their Ni-H.52s. Once on patrol, the aircraft were bounced by three enemy fighters and teniente Rodríguez was wounded. Force-landing near Tardienta, the Republican pilot was helped by militiamen to a field hospital. On the Nationalist side, a three-strong Breguet 19 *patrulla* that was attacked by Herguido and Roig was forced to land at Tardienta frontline airfield.

Both the *Consejería de Defensa* communiqué in Barcelona and the press coverage of this combat were remarkable. According to the first communiqué, 'In the Tardienta area our airmen scored a great success by shooting down three enemy aeroplanes'. The second communiqué added details;

'In the Huesca area rebel forces have carried out strong attacks, escorted by their aircraft which have been battered. Three of our fighter aircraft have shot down two enemy bombers and one fighter.'

A third communiqué admitted that it was the enemy Ni-H.52s – three actually – that had attacked the friendly aircraft;

García Herguido listens to his CO, comandante Alfonso de los Reyes, at Sariñena following the completion of an eventful combat mission in their Ni-H.52s

'A republican Aviation *patrulla* was attacked by six enemy aeroplanes when it was returning from Huesca. Our airmen forced an enemy aircraft down and it was captured by the Tardienta militias. Both the aircraft and the aviator are foreign.'

The Catalan press published additional details;

'Our airmen chased a rebel bomber and forced it down at the village of La Zaida. The pilot was taken prisoner and the aircraft was captured intact by our troops, together with all the crew.'

As we have seen, however, the outcome of this clash was quite different from the official version. Teniente Adonis Rodríguez was the captured 'foreign airman' referred to by the communiqué! Coronel Felipe Díaz Sandino, *Consejero de Defensa* of the Catalan autonomous government, seemed well versed in the techniques of propaganda and disinformation.

By early November 1936 Herguido, promoted to teniente in October, had been sent to the Madrid front. On 17 December, while attached to the Soviet 2ª *Patrulla* of the I-15 *escuadrilla* under Soviet capitán Pavel Vasilievich Richagov (pseudonym 'Palancar'), he suffered a knee wound in a combat over the Madrid front. He managed to land his *Chato* behind friendly lines and was admitted to hospital in Barcelona, where he remained for some days. Upon recovering from his wounds, Herguido rejoined his unit but he was killed in combat with *Legion Condor* He 51s over the Madrid front on 6 January 1937. His friend García La Calle reported;

'In the other Russian *escuadrilla* my friend and comrade Jesús García Herguido, who had just joined because I had called him in, was killed when shot down. According to the commissar, Herguido shot down a Heinkel, which practically crashed on Barajas airfield, but his aeroplane was so close to the Heinkel that he did not have time to recover from a steep dive before he too crashed.'

That day, the He 51s flown by Leutnant Hans-Peter von Gallera and Unteroffizier Kurt Kneiding were shot down and both men killed, while Unteroffizier Walter Leyerer's Heinkel sustained a dozen hits and turned over on landing.

Jesús García Herguido was posthumously promoted to the rank of capitán effective from the date of his death, 6 January 1937.

REPUBLICAN *ESCUADRA DE CAZA* Nº 11

In early September 1937 the so-called *Agrupación de Caza* (Fighter Force) was officially established under the recently-promoted mayor Ramón Puparelli, whose *Plana Mayor* (Staff) was based at Caspe airfield. The following month the first two Spanish I-16 *Mosca* units, the 1ª and 4ª *Escuadrillas* of *Grupo* Nº 21, were established, as was I-15 *Chato*-equipped 2ª *Escuadrilla* of *Grupo* Nº 26, also with Spanish pilots. The *Agrupación de Caza* duly became the *Escuadra de Caza* Nº 11, and it remained under Puparelli's formal command despite actual command being with the Soviets. It should be noted that four *escuadrillas* of *Grupo* Nº 21 and one of *Grupo* Nº 26 still had Soviet personnel and remained under direct Soviet control.

After the fall of the Northern front to the Nationalists, Spanish I-15 *Chato*-equipped 3ª *Escuadrilla* was established at Figueras airfield, in Gerona. Commanded by teniente Juan Comas Borrás, it was comprised of the surviving pilots from that front. Another Spanish unit was soon formed, 4ª *Escuadrilla* being led by teniente Ladislao Duarte Espés.

During the battle of Teruel in December 1937 more pilots began arriving from the USSR, making it possible to create new fighter units. In April 1938 the I-16 *Mosca*-equipped 3ª *Escuadrilla* was re-established under teniente José María Bravo Fernández. Gradually, all the government fighter *escuadrillas* with both *Moscas* and *Chatos* eventually came under wholly Spanish control during the battle of the Ebro. A 7ª *Escuadrilla* was even established within *Grupo* Nº 21, commanded by teniente José Puig Torres. Although the 2ª and 5ª *Escuadrillas* of this *grupo* were equipped with monoplanes – the 5ª with Soviet crews – they were merged in September 1938 and placed under the control of Spanish officer teniente Julio Pereiro Pérez.

Escuadra de Caza Nº 11 was successively led by mayores Ramón Puparelli Francia, Luis Alonso Vega, Isidoro Jiménez García and Andrés García La Calle. All tried their best to control the unit's activities, but only La Calle had significant experience of fighter operations. The *Jefatura* (Staff) of *Escuadra* Nº 11 merely acted as the conduit for orders from the *Fuerzas Aéreas* headquarters, of which there were two from April 1938 when government territory was split at the province of Castellón. One headquarters was based at Barcelona and the other at Albacete.

Mayor Andrés García La Calle, the official hero of the government fighter force, tried new methods and tactics and replaced several of the *escuadrilla* COs. Despite these changes, the situation in Spain was irreversible for the Republicans by then and the war was duly lost.

Ramón Puparelli Francia

Born at Sucelle, in Salamanca, on 8 November 1898, Ramón Puparelli Francia joined the Artillery Corps in February 1919. On 6 June 1925 sargento Puparelli was enrolled in the combined air gunnery and bombardier course at Los Alcázares, and was subsequently posted to de Havilland DH 4-equipped 3ª *Escuadrilla* of 3º *Grupo* of the 2ª *Escuadra* at Melilla. He participated in operations in Morocco until 1927. The following year, and now a Suboficial de Artillería, Puparelli took a military pilot's course from which he graduated in October 1928. He was posted to the *Grupo de Instrucción* at Getafe and later to Cuatro Vientos.

There were further promotions, to alférez in 1934 and teniente in 1935, before Puparelli was posted to 3ª *Escuadrilla* of *Grupo de Reconocimiento* Nº 21 at León. Within days of the outbreak of the civil war he was posted to the *Escuadrilla de Experimentación en Vuelo de los Servicios Técnicos* (Technical Branch Air Test Squadron) at Cuatro Vientos. Puparelli soon started flying sorties in Breguet 19s, Ni-H.52s and D.372s, as well as the sole Boeing 281 monoplane demonstrator at Cuatro Vientos, which was awaiting return to its manufacturer in the USA at the time. He was one of the pilots who bombed the Alcázar in Toledo in July 1936.

On 2 August Puparelli flew a reconnaissance mission over the San Rafael-Ávila, Navacerrada and Alto del León roads in a Breguet 19, dropping bombs on the pine forests. The following day he bombed an enemy battery at Alto del León. A short while later he was deployed to Don Benito and Herrera del Duque airfields in Extremadura, where he led Ni-H.52 fighter *patrulla* – the pilots under his command were García La Calle, Alonso Santamaría and Peña Dugo. During this period of operations the Republican pilots engaged He 51s, which were clearly superior to the government-owned Nieuport fighters.

Puparelli was soon back at Getafe flying Breguet 19s, attacking the Sierra and Talavera de la Reina fronts. On 2 September he targeted the village of San Rafael, in Segovia. Later, accompanying capitán Manuel Cascón, he used a D.372 to down a He 51 over the Madrid front. This earned Puparelli promotion to capitán, and he was also made CO of all Republican fighter units on the Madrid front.

On 21 October a shortage of fighters in the Madrid area forced Puparelli to scramble in the Boeing 281, and he fell victim to Nationalist CR.32s between Pinto and Parla. Bailing out successfully, he broke ribs on landing and spent the next few months recovering in hospital in Madrid. By February 1937 Puparelli was well enough to be given command of the first two Spanish I-15 *escuadrillas*. Following enemy air raids on the power stations in Catalonia, capitán Alonso Santamaría's 2ª *Escuadrilla*

Teniente Ramón Puparelli Francia, wearing sunglasses and standing immediately below the propeller hub, poses with mechanics and militiamen in front of a D.372

was ordered to Lérida airfield on 20 February. *Grupo de Caza* CO capitán Puparelli oversaw the unit's move, 2ª *Escuadrilla* flying eight of its I-15s to Lérida on the 21st so as to protect the power stations at Tremp and Camarasa.

In March Puparelli moved to Alcalá de Henares airfield, where he led *Grupo de Caza* Nº 16 during operations around Guadalajara. In early July he was ordered to take his I-15s to Santander to reinforce the northern fighter force. There, he assumed command of both an I-15 and I-16 *escuadrilla*. Directing operations on the Biscay, Asturias and Santander fronts in July and August, Puparelli was promoted to mayor de Artillería during this period. Just prior to the fall of Santander on 25 August, he returned to the central area in a Douglas DC-2.

In September Puparelli took command of the *Agrupación de Caza*, which became *Escuadra de Caza* Nº 11 in October. He participated in operations over the Aragon front, flying alongside his staff pilots from Caspe airfield. In February 1938 Puparelli handed over command of *Escuadra* Nº 11 to mayor Luis Alonso Vega, having been appointed CO of the 4ª *Región Aérea*, with his headquarters in Valencia. He remained here until 5 May, when he was relieved by coronel Felipe Díaz Sandino and given command of the 3ª *Sección* (Operations) of the *Estado Mayor de Fuerzas Aéreas* in Barcelona. On 26 October Puparelli was appointed chief-of-staff of the *Estado Mayor de Fuerzas Aéreas* in the Northern Zone. It was in November 1938, during that posting, that he was promoted to teniente coronel de Artillería (lieutenant colonel).

After the fall of Catalonia in January 1939, Puparelli escaped to France, where he was interned in a concentration camp. He eventually left for exile in Argentina, but no further information is available on his subsequent life.

Now a capitán, balding Puparelli (in white overalls) eats with maestre Juan Comas Borrás (wearing a flying cap) to his right. At the time this photograph was taken Puparelli was CO of the short-lived I-15-equipped *Grupo* Nº 16, which consisted of La Calle's and Alonso Santamaría's *escuadrillas*

Capitán Puparelli and the pilots of the I-15 *Escuadrilla de Chatos del Norte* at La Albericia in August 1937. Standing, from left to right, are Fernando Villins León, sargento Román Llorente Castro, unidentified, unidentified, capitán Ramón Puparelli Francia (*grupo* CO, white overalls), unidentified, unidentified and sargentos Ladislao Duarte Espés, Miguel Zambudio Martínez and José Rubert Tomás. Squatting, from left to right, are sargentos Andrés Rodríguez Panadero and José Recalde Gómez, teniente Jaime Buyé Berni, Nicomedes Calvo Aguilar, unidentified, unidentified and sargentos Antonio Miró Vidal and Miguel Galindo Saura. After leaving the 6ª *Región Aérea*, Puparelli was appointed commander of the whole *Escuadra de Caza* (Republican fighter force)

Luis Alonso Vega

Having joined the *Escuela de Aeronáutica Naval* in Barcelona in 1924, Alonso Vega graduated as a pilot of land-based aircraft at the *Escuela Civil* in Albacete and later as a floatplane pilot in Barcelona. He was promoted to segundo contramaeste in July 1931 and flew Savoia S.62 EA-BAA on a number of occasions. Shortly afterwards, however, Alonso Vega was posted to the *Escuadrilla de Caza Martinsyde*, and remained with the 1ª *Patrulla* until 1932.

Upon the establishment of the new *Cuerpo de Auxiliares de Aeronáutica Naval* (Naval Air Corps Reserve) he was promoted to auxiliar segundo, alférez de fragata in March 1932 and auxiliar primero on 23 November. In 1933 Alonso Vega served with the *Servicio Fotográfico*, flying Hispano-Suiza E-30 EA-HAA, and the following year he was posted to the 2ª *Patrulla* of the *Escuadrilla de Bombardeo*. Based at San Javier, this unit was equipped with six Dornier Wal flying boats.

In the months prior to the civil war Alonso Vega joined the 1ª *Patrulla* of the 3ª *Escuadrilla de Reconocimiento*, and on 18 May 1936 he detached to Mahón, in Minorca, where he flew Savoia S.62 flying boats. Once the conflict started Alonso Vega participated in the landing operations on Majorca. Promoted to the rank of *oficial segundo* (lieutenant), he was then transferred to the 1ª *Escuadrilla Mixta* of *Grupo* Nº 21, based at Albacete and Andújar. There, he flew Ni-H.52s as escorts for Breguet 19s on the Andalusia front. On 9 October Alonso Vega engaged a CR.32 *patrulla*, but his Nieuport '3-28' suffered damage to its engine and fuel tank. Bleeding from a leg wound, Alonso Vega force landed in a field 14 miles (22 km) from Montoro, in Córdoba, and was taken to the local field hospital.

Having recovered from his wounds, he was promoted to capitán in December 1936 and posted as an instructor to the *Escuela Elemental* at La Ribera on 8 March 1937. This order was cancelled four days later, however. The first Polikarpov R-Z *Natacha* biplane reconnaissance bombers arrived in Spain in late February 1937, and towards the end of the following month Alonso Vega was posted to the 1ª *Escuadrilla* of *Grupo* Nº 20, which was equipped with these aircraft. He subsequently participated in the battle of Guadalajara in an R-Z in March. On 8 May Alonso Vega led an unsuccessful attempt to move his *escuadrilla* to the

Auxiliar 1º Luis Alonso Vega of the *Aeronáutica Naval* had flown Martinsyde F 4s before the war, but he found himself flying Savoia S.62 seaplane fighters at Mahón, in Minorca, during the early stages of the conflict. He was soon ordered to reinforce *Grupo* Nº 11, which was equipped with Ni-H.52s at Andújar – one of its machines is seen here being refuelled between missions

north via France, but the unit ended up being stopped by French authorities at Toulouse airfield. Back in Spain by June, he and his *escuadrilla* participated in the Huesca offensive. Several aircraft were lost during the campaign.

Following the disbandment of *Grupo* Nº 20 and his promotion to mayor in August 1937, Alonso Vega was appointed to command *Grupo de Natachas* Nº 30. He led the unit between 6 August 1937

and 20 February 1938, when he was succeeded by mayor de Aviación Naval Valentín Pelayo Berra. Alonso Vega was appointed CO of the *Escuadra de Caza* Nº 11 shortly thereafter, which he commanded during the retreat from Aragon and in the fighting in Levante. Based with his staff at Valls airfield, in Tarragona, Alonso Vega participated in the first phase of the battle of the Ebro in August-September 1938.

On 24 September he handed over command of the *Escuadra de Caza* Nº 11 to mayor Isidoro Jiménez, after which Alonso Vega headed up the *Fuerzas Aéreas* staff of the Central-Southern area, based at Finca de Los Llanos. Promoted to teniente coronel de Aviación on 11 December 1938, he served under coronel Antonio Camacho, Chief-of-Staff of the *Zona Aérea Centro-Sur*. At the end of the war Alonso Vega flew to Oran, in Algeria, where he was interned until he moved to Mexico. No further information on his later life has come to light.

Isidoro Jiménez García

Born at Valladolid on 8 April 1899, Isidoro Jiménez García volunteered for service with the *Regimiento de Ferrocarriles* (Railway Regiment) in 1918. He was promoted to cabo the following year and, in 1920, to sargento de Ingenieros (Engineer Corps). In 1925 Isidoro Jiménez attended the aerial gunnery/bombardier course at Los Alcázares. On graduation he was posted to the *Base de Hidros* at El Atalayón, in Melilla, to fly reconnaissance and bombing missions in Morocco.

In 1928 Isidoro Jiménez took a flying course for NCOs and was promoted to suboficial de Ingenieros. He was then posted to Madrid to join *Escuadra* Nº 1 at Getafe airfield, where he remained until March 1933. Isidoro Jiménez then reported to Cuatro Vientos for a mechanics' course, which he completed in December, and was then given priority for the next vacant fighter unit posting. In July 1934 Isidoro Jiménez was promoted to subteniente (sub-lieutenant), but remained with the Breguet 19-equipped 2ª *Escuadrilla* of *Grupo de Reconocimiento* Nº 31 at Getafe. In December 1935 he was promoted to alférez.

Soon after the outbreak of the war Isidoro Jiménez flew a reconnaissance mission over the main roads leading to Madrid, flying as far as Burgos. He subsequently undertook further reconnaissance and bombing sorties over the Sierra de Madrid and Alcázar de Toledo. On 14 August Isidoro Jiménez, who had been promoted to capitán de Ingenieros the previous month, was deployed to Sariñena to lead a three-aircraft

While flying a Ni-H.52 similar to this one, Alonso Vega was wounded in combat over the Córdoba front. He later commanded the Polikarpov R-Z *Natacha*-equipped *Grupo* Nº 20 before relieving Puparelli as leader of the *Escuadra de Caza*

At the start of the war Isidoro Jiménez flew Breguet 19 bombers followed by Polikarpov R-Zs. He was then sent on a training course in the USSR, where he learned to fly the I-16. Upon his return to Spain Jiménez was appointed commander of the I-16 *Escuela de Alta Velocidad* school at El Carmolí, in Murcia

Despite being in his late 30s, mayor Isidoro Jiménez quickly found himself at home in the cockpit of the I-16 *Mosca*

During the battle of the Ebro, Jiménez replaced Alonso Vega as leader of the *Escuadra de Caza*, remaining in this position until December 1938

Breguet 19 *patrulla*. Shortly thereafter he became CO of the mixed Breguet 19/Ni-H.52 *Escuadrilla 'Alas Rojas'*, which also included some de Havilland DH 84 Dragons and DH 89 Dragon Rapides within its ranks. While Isidoro Jiménez was at Sariñena the first I-15 *patrulla*, led by prominent Soviet pilot Ivan Kopets, arrived on the Aragon front.

In late December 1936 he was selected to go to the USSR together with comandante Manuel Cascón and capitanes Aurelio Villimar, José González Montero, Gumersindo Areán and 200 other pilots. Returning to Spain in July 1937, Isidoro Jiménez participated in the battle of Brunete that same month. He commanded the R-Z *Natacha*-equipped 50ª *Escuadrilla*, which operated from airfields at Talamanca del Jarama and Santa Cruz de la Zarza. In August he moved with the *escuadrilla* to Villar del Arzobispo and then to Barcelona, remaining there until the unit's disbandment in September.

In October 1937 Isidoro Jiménez became an instructor at the *Escuelas de Vuelo* and succeeded mayor Félix Sampil as CO of the *Escuela de Caza* at El Carmolí, in Murcia. There, he was a member of the first I-16 course. Isidoro Jiménez was promoted to mayor de Aviación in June 1938, and three months later he succeeded mayor Luis Alonso Vega as CO of the *Escuadra de Caza* Nº 11 – a posting he retained for much of the battle of the Ebro (July to November 1938), the civil war's bloodiest campaign. Based at Valls, Isidoro Jiménez led several sorties over the front in one of two I-15s assigned to the staff flight of *Escuadra* Nº 11.

During the early days of the campaign in Catalonia, he handed over command of the unit to mayor Andrés García La Calle and returned to the *Escuela de Alta Velocidad* at El Carmolí as CO. Isidoro Jiménez was still there at war's end, being captured by the Nationalists. Isidoro Jiménez subsequently died in Madrid.

Andrés García La Calle

Born in Sestao, Biscay, on 4 February 1909, Andrés García La Calle gained a private pilot's licence at the Madrid Aero Club in 1929. In October of that year he was admitted to the *Escuela de Vuelo y Combate* at Alcalá de Henares. He later attended the *Escuela de Transformación* (Transitional School) at Guadalajara, from which he graduated as a military pilot. García La Calle was initially posted to Auamara, in Larache, then to the *Escuela de Observadores* (Observers' School) at Cuatro Vientos and, finally, to the *Escuela de Tiro y Bombardeo* at Los Alcázares. There, he flew DH 9s, before moving in 1932 to Loring R-III-equipped *Grupo de Reconocimiento* Nº 22 in Seville. García La Calle was promoted to sargento piloto in 1934.

When the civil war commenced he was a member of the 2ª *Escuadrilla* of the *Grupo de Caza* Nº 11, which flew Ni-H.52s from Getafe. García La Calle distinguished himself in the early engagements over the Sierra de Madrid by shooting down several Nationalist aircraft and logging an impressive 82 flying hours in the second half of July alone. During this time the future ace flew Ni-H.52s, D.372s and Loire 46 C1s with the government's *Aviación Militar*. Later, García La Calle was detached to Herrera del Duque and Don Benito airfields on the Extremadura front.

Subsquently flying a Hawker Spanish Fury over the Talavera de la Reina area against Nationalist CR.32s and Ju 52/3ms, García La Calle was promoted to alférez in September 1936 and continued flying the last remaining fighters available in Madrid until 28 October, when he left for Barcelona on leave. In November he was posted to a Soviet *escuadrilla* equipped with I-15s, its CO being future ace Pavel Rychagov, who flew under the pseudonym 'Palancar'. From the 6th García La Calle flew combat missions over Madrid, initially as a wingman in the *patrulla* led by Soviet pilot Ivan ('José') Kopets. Later, he became *patrulla* CO after 'José' assumed command of the *Escuadrilla Rychagov* when Rychagov was removed from frontline duties. Soviet sources credit García La Calle with an aerial victory during this period.

Promoted to teniente in November 1936 and to capitán two months later, García La Calle was subsequently given command of the first Spanish I-15 *escuadrilla*, which included an American *patrulla*. This unit, called the *Escuadrilla 'La Calle'*, initially comprised three elements. The 1ª *Patrulla* consisted of García La Calle, José Calderón, Ramón Castañeda and American Ben Leider (aka 'Lando'), the 2ª *Patrulla* comprised Jim Allison, Frank Tinker ('Gómez Trejo'), Harold 'Whitey' Dahl and José 'Chang' Sellés and the 3ª *Patrulla* was made up of Luis Bercial, Esteban Ortiz, José Riverola and Gerardo Gil.

The *escuadrilla* arrived at the old Hispano-Suiza factory airfield at Guadalajara on 7 February, just in time to participate in the battle of the Jarama. It achieved considerable success during this campaign, which lasted until 27 February, but suffered heavy losses in the process. José Calderón, Ben Leider and Luis Bercial were killed, while Jim Allison and Harold Dahl were shot down but survived. According to Tinker, by the time the Jarama battle ended García La Calle had been credited with 11 victories. The American ace rated him a good CO, but future ace Tarazona and veteran fighter leader Sayós, both of whom later came under his command, did not share this opinion.

Capitán García La Calle was, chronologically, the second 'official hero' of the Republican fighter force, being credited with 11 aerial victories

García La Calle was assigned Spanish Fury '4-1', this photograph showing the aircraft after it had been overhauled and camouflaged in Alicante in 1937 – it was flown in silver by La Calle in 1936

The so-called *Escuadrilla La Calle* made its debut in the battle of the Jarama. They are, standing, from left to right, Harold 'Whitey' Dahl, José 'Chang' Sellés, unidentified, García La Calle (*escuadrilla* CO), Gerardo Gil and Ramón Castañeda. The groundcrew are wearing black berets

During the battle of Guadalajara the *Escuadrilla La Calle* welcomed new pilots. Posing in this photograph, again standing, from left to right, are Frank Tinker, Francisco Escapa (mechanic), José Riverola Grúas, Gerardo Gil Sánchez, Ramón Castañeda Pardo, García La Calle (*escuadrilla* CO) and Eusebio Fernández de Velasco. Squatting, from left to right, are José Bastida Porres, Harold Dahl, José 'Chang' Sellés and Augusto Lecha

Mayor Andrés García La Calle, with his back to the camera and wearing an officer's cap at right, had taken command of the *Escuadra de Caza* by late December 1938. He is seen here talking to capitán José María Bravo, the second CO of *Grupo N° 21 de 'Moscas'*, and other *escuadrilla* COs

The unit also participated in the battle of Guadalajara in March, during which *Escuadrilla La Calle* suffered the loss of teniente piloto Antonio Blanch Latorre of the *Aeronáutica Naval*. Guatemalan pilot Manuel García Gómez was also shot down, although he survived in Nationalist hands and was later returned in a prisoner exchange. Following the conclusion of the battle on 23 March, García La Calle was succeeded by capitán Jiménez Bruguet for a short period. The *escuadrilla* fought on the Teruel front from early April through to 24 May, when new CO teniente José Riverola led the unit from El Soto to Bilbao, on the Northern front.

On 20 June capitán García La Calle went to the Soviet Union as an accompanying instructor for the second pilots' course. The party crossed into France at Port Bou and sailed for the USSR aboard the French ship SS *Téophile Gautier*. Following hospital treatment for a minor heart ailment once in the Soviet Union, García La Calle was sent to No 20 Pilots' School, which had been established to train Spanish aviators at Kirovabad (now Ganja) in the northern Caucasus. He commanded it jointly with a Soviet officer.

García La Calle returned to Spain on 3 March 1938. After a series of Nationalist raids on Barcelona, he was placed in charge of the air defences of both the city and nearby coastal region. In May he was ordered to form the *Grupo* N° 28, which was equipped with Canadian Car & Foundry-built Grumman GE-23 *Delfín* biplanes that were to be used for ground attack and coastal patrol duties. As CO, García La Calle participated in the early stages of the battle of the Ebro, although in reality he did little flying as he was attached to the command post of general Rojo and coronel Modesto as *Aviación* liaison officer. Later, he operated with his unit over the Eastern front at Lérida from August.

In October 1938 García La Calle handed over command of the *Grupo de Grumman* to mayor Antonio Saluela Lucientes, having been appointed deputy CO of the *Escuadra de Caza* N° 11. He took command of the unit during the battle of Catalonia on 22 December, having been promoted to mayor the previous month. His predecessor, mayor Isidoro Jiménez, had in turn been posted to the *Jefatura* of the *Escuela de Alta Velocidad* at El Carmolí.

On 6 February 1939 García La Calle flew his last sortie when he was ordered to evacuate Vilajuiga airfield, in Gerona. He landed his *Chato* at Francazal airfield, in Toulouse, and went into exile in France. After questioning by *Armée de l'Air* officers, he sailed for Mexico. Initially spending time in the Dominican Republic, García La Calle returned to settle in Mexico. Here, he wrote one of the earliest and most popular – if somewhat unbalanced – memoirs of a Spanish Republican fighter pilot, entitled *Mitos y verdades; la aviación de caza en la guerra española*. García La Calle died in Mexico in 1976.

REPUBLICAN FIGHTER FORCE IN THE NORTH

The first fighters to arrive on the Northern front were two Ni-H.52s flown from Barcelona by sargento Emilio Villaceballos and teniente Amador Silverio Jiménez. These aircraft were not reinforced until November 1936, when 15 I-15 *Chatos* were shipped to Santander aboard the SS *A Andreyev*, together with their Soviet pilots and groundcrew. These fighters subsequently flew from Carreño airfield (Gijón) on the Asturias front. During their first sortie, the I-15 pilots claimed to have shot down an enemy Fokker F.XII tri-motor and a Heinkel He 46, although both aircraft – which had indeed suffered battle damage – managed to land at Navia airfield.

The *Chatos* also participated in the offensive at Villareal de Álava in December 1936, and by year-end the Soviet pilots had been joined by Spanish aviators teniente Juan Roldán and alférez Felipe del Río Crespo. The latter made his first claim on 28 December, but teniente Roldán was shot down flying I-15 '15' during an engagement involving German-flown He 51s over Bilbao on 4 January 1937.

In March further fighters arrived by sea when eight Czech Letov Š.231s were delivered to the Northern front aboard the SS *Sarkani*. After a call for volunteers to fly them, a group of pilots were flown in aboard a DC-2 on 23 March. The new arrivals included Baquedano Moreno, Barbero López, Lambás Bernal, González Feo, Sánchez de las Matas, Rodríguez Panadero, Rodríguez de la Cueva, Olmos Genovés and García Borrajo. The Letovs, however, proved a disappointment. Several turned over on landing before they were even operational, one was shot down on its first sortie (and sargento piloto Juan Olmos captured) and several others were set on fire during an air raid.

The second loss of a Spanish *Chato* pilot was recorded on 15 April when sargento José Rodríguez de la Cueva was shot down near Vitoria by Italian CR.32s. On the 22nd *escuadrilla* CO capitán Felipe del Río Crespo was killed when his *Chato* fell victim to German-flown Bf 109s over Bilbao. His successor, teniente Tomás Baquedano, was also shot down by Bf 109s on

Personnel of the I-15 *Escuadrilla de Chatos del Norte* on the Northern front in 1937. They are, from left to right, sargentos Miguel Zambudio Martínez and Andrés Rodríguez Panadero, tenientes José González Feo and Tomás Baquedano Moreno and capitán Antonio Sánchez de las Matas

This Northern front photograph was taken at La Albericia airfield, in Santander, in 1937. Posing for the camera alongside an unidentified I-15 are, from left to right, tenientes Miguel San José Andrade and Juan Comas Borrás, sargentos Miguel Zambudio Martínez and Andrés Rodríguez Panadero and tenientes José González Feo and Leopoldo Morquillas Rubio

28 May while defending Santander. He bailed out but was fired on while in his parachute and died in Santander's Valdecilla hospital.

In May two further *Chato* formations made non-stop flights to Santander. One, of six aircraft led by teniente Gerardo Gil, arrived on the 22nd. They were joined two days later by another ten aircraft under the command of teniente José Riverola. On 2 July a further ten fighters arrived, led by the *Grupo de Chatos* CO capitán Ramón Puparelli. Four more under the command of teniente Juan Comas Borrás joined soon afterwards, so that 45 *Chatos* were now available for operations on the Northern front. They were subsequently reinforced by eight Soviet-flown I-16 *Moscas* led by Valentin Ukhov.

Following Riverola's departure for the Central front, teniente Morquillas was appointed CO of the *Escuadrilla de Chatos del Norte*. The unit was comprised of the following pilots and aircraft during operations on the Santander front in July 1937;

Unit	Pilot	Aircraft type/code
1ª *Patrulla*	Teniente Leopoldo Morquillas Rubio	I-15 '57'
	Teniente Jaime Buyé Berni	I-15 '35'
	Teniente Nicomedes Calvo Aguilar	I-15 '29'
	Sargento Rafael Magriñá Vidal	I-15 '13'
2ª *Patrulla*	Teniente Esteban Nazario Ortiz Bueno	I-15 '12'
	Teniente Miguel San José Andrade	I-15 '50'
	Sargento Miguel Galindo Saura	I-15 '28'
	Sargento Andrés Rodríguez Panadero	I-15 '20'
3ª *Patrulla*	Teniente Juan Comas Borrás	I-15 '59'
	Teniente José González Feo	I-15 '30'
	Sargento Miguel Zambudio Martínez	I-15 '62'
	Sargento Ladislao Duarte Espés	I-15 '23'
Reserve pilots	Teniente Julián Barbero López	
	Sargento Antonio Rodríguez Jordán	
	Sargento Antonio Miró Vidal	
	Sargento Román Llorente Castro	

On 17 August 1937 a nine-strong I-16 *escuadrilla* led by future ace, and Hero of the Soviet Union, Snr Lt Boris Smirnov arrived at La Albericia airfield, in Santander, from Alcalá de Henares. The unit was comprised of the following pilots;

Snr Lt Boris Smirnov (*Escuadrilla* CO)
Sargento Eloy Gonzalo Obarro (later killed in action)
Sargento Luis de Frutos González
Sargento Tomás Saladrigas Guardia (later wounded in action)
Sargento Antonio Pardo Iglesias (later killed in action)
Sargento Francisco Tarazona Torán (later wounded in action)
Sargento Juan Huertas García
Sargento Daniel Ranz Díaz de Artacoz (later killed in action)
Sargento Restituto Félix Toquero Burillo

During the campaigns in Santander and Asturias many pilots were killed, wounded or reported missing. The government airmen had to fight under conditions of clear inferiority, mainly due to the lack of strength in depth and also because their airfields were systematically bombed, with heavy losses both in men and materiel. After the Republican defeat on the Asturias front, the *Chatos* flown by Duarte and Llorente, as well as Luis de Frutos' *Mosca*, were the only fighters that managed to escape to France on 20 October 1937. In total, 43 I-15s and 16 I-16s had been lost during the campaign.

Felipe del Río Crespo

Born at Nueva Montaña, in Santander, on 9 September 1912, Felipe del Río Crespo subsequently studied for an engineering degree. As the holder of a private pilot's licence issued in October 1933, he joined the air force at Cuatro Vientos upon being called up for military service. Del Río Crespo commenced his elementary training as a reserve military pilot flying de Havilland DH 60 Moth Majors, and graduated as a cabo. He undertook his advanced training on outdated DH 9s, graduating near the top of his class in June 1934. Together with classmates Arístides García López and Manuel Izquierdo, del Río Crespo took part in the Spanish *Vuelta Aérea* (Air Tour), flying a DH 60 from Alcalá, before participating in an airshow at Barajas that was attended by the president of the Republic. Del Río Crespo was subsequently selected for the team of the *Escuela de Vuelo*, which went to Lisbon for an international airshow.

In July 1935, he was promoted to sargento de complement (Reserve Sargeant), after which he was discharged. The outbreak of the civil war found him in Bilbao and, as a military pilot, del Río Crespo reported to the government authorities. He flew civilian light aircraft from Lamiaco airfield and dropped leaflets on the rebel-held barracks at Loyola, in San Sebastián. On one of these flights he crashed, writing his aircraft off.

After a short spell of re-training at Alcalá de Henares, del Río Crespo returned to the Northern front. He initially flew as an air gunner and bombardier in de Havilland DH 85 Leopard Moth light aircraft that had been pressed into military service, and also in Breguet 19 '12-83' flown by brigada José Rivera. Later, del Río Crespo flew Breguet 19 '12-107',

Studio portrait of sargento Felipe del Río Crespo wearing his military uniform as a pilot of the *Aviación Militar*

and in September he was sent to La Albericia airfield and then to Carreño to fly sorties on the Santander and Oviedo fronts. His pilot throughout this period was sargento piloto Benjamín Gutiérrez Junco and their Breguet 19 was coded '12-202'. Del Río Crespo also flew with cabos ametralladores-bombarderos Eduardo Tornil Estada, Antonio Silvano Rodríguez and Gumersindo Gutiérrez Merino.

In October 1936 del Río Crespo was promoted to sargento and sent to serve with comandante Alfredo Sanjuán, chief of staff in the North. By late November, and following the arrival of the I-15s led by Soviet pilots Boris Turzhanskiy and K A Baranchuk, brigada del Río Crespo converted onto the *Chato* along with teniente piloto Juan Roldán Maldonado. Both men participated in combat over the Alava front at Villarreal during the failed offensive on Vitoria in December 1936. Del Río Crespo's first confirmed aerial victory was recorded on the 28th of that month when he attacked a DH 89 Dragon Rapide, scoring 200 hits on the enemy aircraft and wounding the observer. Despite the damage, however, the crippled aircraft managed to limp back to Lasarte airfield, in San Sebastián. Del Río Crespo also took part in the defence of Bilbao on 3-4 January 1937, during which his comrade teniente Juan Roldán perished when his I-15 was downed by He 51s. On a more positive note, del Río Crespo was credited with shooting down one of the attacking Ju 52/3ms near Bilbao on the 4th.

On 22 March 1937 del Río Crespo was promoted to teniente. That same month a group of Spanish pilots arrived in Santander to fly the recently acquired Š.231s, although Tenientes Tomás Baquedano, Leopoldo Morquillas and Julián Barbero and sargento Andrés Rodríguez Panadero were attached to the *Chato escuadrilla*.

During the Biscay campaign the pilots of the *Escuadrilla de Chatos del Norte*, now led by teniente del Río Crespo, distinguished themselves in combat over Bilbao on 13 and 18 April 1937. The unit claimed to have shot down three of the attackers, but only one of the new Dornier Do 17

Instructors and student pilots of the *Curso de Pilotos Militares de Complemento* (Reserve Pilot Course) at Alcalá de Henares, in Madrid, in 1935. Felipe del Río Crespo is sixth from the left in the back row

twin-engined bombers of the *Legion Condor* crashed in government territory on the 18th – its demise was credited to del Río Crespo. He had also claimed an unidentified German bomber destroyed three five days earlier. Del Río Crespo had been promoted to capitán following his success on the 13th. On 20 April he and his unit accounted for the Breguet 19 flown by capitán José Antonio del Val Núñez, who was seriously wounded and forced to land near Azpeitia.

This photograph was taken at the burial ceremony for capitán Felipe del Río Crespo at Guecho, in Bilbao, in late April 1937. At left, wearing suits, are his father and brother, Manuel. In uniform second from the right is teniente coronel de Aviación Ismael Warleta, who was the air force's Leading Armament Officer at the time

Two days later, over Bilbao, the *Chato* flown by del Río Crespo was bounced by Bf 109s from 2.J/88 and the ace was shot down and killed.

Some historians state that he had been shot down by gunfire from the government destroyer *José Luis Díez*, moored in Bilbao harbour. That is completely false. The three pilots flying with del Río Crespo, tenientes Julián Barbero, José González Feo and Leopoldo Morquillas, stated categorically that their commander had fallen victim to Bf 109s. Barbero avoided being shot down by the German fighters by tricking his opponents into thinking that his aircraft had been terminally damaged, although he was able to land at Lamiaco. No operational reports of the *Fuerzas Aéreas del Norte* from that day had come to light until, by chance, the author found the following documentation to prove what had happened;

'At 1600 hrs a flight patrolling near the airfield sighted nine twin-engined bombers and several fighters heading for Bilbao. The government aircraft forced them into combat lasting 20 minutes and shot down two enemy fighters. One was a Heinkel and the other was unknown. In this combat one aircraft was lost.'

That aircraft was the I-15 flown by capitán Felipe del Río Crespo. His posthumous promotion to mayor was dated 22 April 1937 – the day of his death.

Andrés Rodríguez Panadero

Born at San Martín de la Vega, in Madrid, on 30 November 1916, Andrés Rodríguez Panadero worked as a mechanic before volunteering for service in the *Arma de Aviación Militar* in February 1935. He was posted to the *Escuadra* Nº 1 at Getafe and assigned to the *Escuadrilla de Plana Mayor* (Staff Flight). On 1 July 1936 Panadero joined the 1ª *Escuadrilla* of the *Grupo de Reconocimiento* Nº 31 as a soldado de 1ª (Private First Class). He took part in the IV *Semana Gimnástica Deportiva Militar* (5th Military Sporting Week) to earn himself a month's leave, which coincided with the start of the civil war.

Panadero duly enrolled in a flying course and graduated in January 1937 as a military pilot with the rank of sargento. Rated suitable for fighters, he was posted to the Northern front on 22 March 1937 and arrived at Santander by air. Joining teniente Felipe del Río's I-15 *Chato Escuadrilla de Caza*, Panadero distinguished himself in the April combats

33

over Bilbao. He shared in the destruction of a Do 17 over the town on the 18th and continued flying I-15s under the command of tenientes Riverola and Morquillas on the Santander and Asturias fronts in July and August. During this period Panadero was assigned I-15 '20' in the 2ª *patrulla*, led by teniente Esteban Ortiz.

Sargento Andrés Rodríguez Panadero was one of the most skilled fighter pilots to serve on the Northern front. For that reason he assumed command of the I-16 *escuadrilla* in the north without any prior conversion training onto the tricky Soviet monoplane fighter

Promoted to teniente in August, he was then posted to the *Escuadrilla I-16 Mosca del Norte*. Panadero's proven flying ability allowed him to convert onto the monoplane without any need for formal instruction on the type. He subsequently took command of the unit when Soviet pilots left the Northern front. Panadero led the *escuadrilla* during the bitter fighting of the Asturias campaign until he was killed when his *Mosca* was shot down in combat with *Legion Condor* Bf 109s from 1.J/88 near Gijón on 28 September 1937 – he had fallen victim to German ace Oberleutnant Harro Harder. The entry for that fateful day in the 6ª *Región Aérea* Operations Record Book noted;

'At 1100 hrs enemy aircraft were detected heading towards Gijón. Four monoplanes and four biplanes were scrambled, which prevented the bombers from reaching Gijón.

A combat ensued with the enemy escort monoplanes, several of which were driven off but others arrived, which our aircraft continued to repel. This combat lasted for an hour. The monoplane flown by the teniente Jefe of the *Escuadrilla*, Andrés Rodríguez Panadero, was shot down in flames. The pilot was killed and the aircraft completely wrecked.'

Rodríguez Panadero was posthumously promoted to the rank of capitán on 26 January 1938.

The *Escuadrilla de Caza del Norte* pilots at La Albericia airfield, in Santander, in May 1937. They are, from left to right, Miguel Zambudio Martínez, Andrés Rodríguez Panadero, Pedro Lambás Bernal, Antonio Sánchez de las Matas, José González Feo, Tomás Baquedano Moreno (*escuadrilla* CO) and two unidentified pilots

Rafael Magriñá Vidal

A graduate of the flying school of the *Dirección General de Aeronáutica*, Rafael Magriñá Vidal was born at Marlloréns on 22 November 1914. He gained his wings in January 1933, and as a pilot was conscripted into the *Arma de Aviación* in February 1936. Posted to the *Fuerzas Aéreas de África* at Tetuán, Magriñá was on leave when the military uprising started. He therefore reported for duty at Canudas airfield, in Barcelona, on 30 July, and that same day flew a DH 87 Hornet Moth light aircraft for the government.

Although only an Aviación private, the *Generalitat de Catalunya* mobilised him as an alférez piloto on 1 August 1936 according to an

An I-16 *Mosca* is serviced in the open on the Northern front. Rafael Magriñá may have been flying this aircraft when he downed Italian ace Guido Presel over Somorrostro, in Biscay, in June 1937

order dated 1 November. Magriñá was sent to the *Escuela de Pilotos* at La Ribera, where he graduated as a sargento Piloto Militar in November 1936 after completing the fighter pilots' course under comandante Félix Sampil. Magriñá was one of the first Spanish reserve pilots selected to fly the I-15, being posted to the 2ª *Escuadrilla*, commanded by capitán Roberto Alonso Santamaría, on the Aragon front in February 1937. Later, he was attached to García La Calle's *escuadrilla* during the battle of Guadalajara.

Flying *Chato* '62', Magriñá headed to the Northern front with teniente Riverola's *escuadrilla* on 24 May, landing at Sondica. He was a *patrulla* CO in the *Escuadrilla de Caza del Norte*, operating over the Biscay front. Flying his I-15, Magriñá managed to shoot down a CR.32 that was strafing Somorrostro airfield on 5 June. The enemy aircraft crashed on a beach between Abanto and Ciérvana, killing Italian ace Tenente Guido Presel.

On 2 July an eight-strong I-16 *escuadrilla* arrived in the North, led by Valentin Ukhov. Later that month newly promited teniente Magriñá was one of three Spanish pilots selected by the Soviet command to fly the *Mosca*. On 17 August, at the start of the offensive in Santander, Magriñá was killed when his I-16 was shot down by enemy fighters at Ciriego.

This Northern front I-16 Type 5 has been jacked up so that repairs can be made to its badly damaged wings and tail unit

I-16 *Mosca* '33' was captured intact by Nationalist troops at the end of the campaign in the north and sent to Germany for evaluation

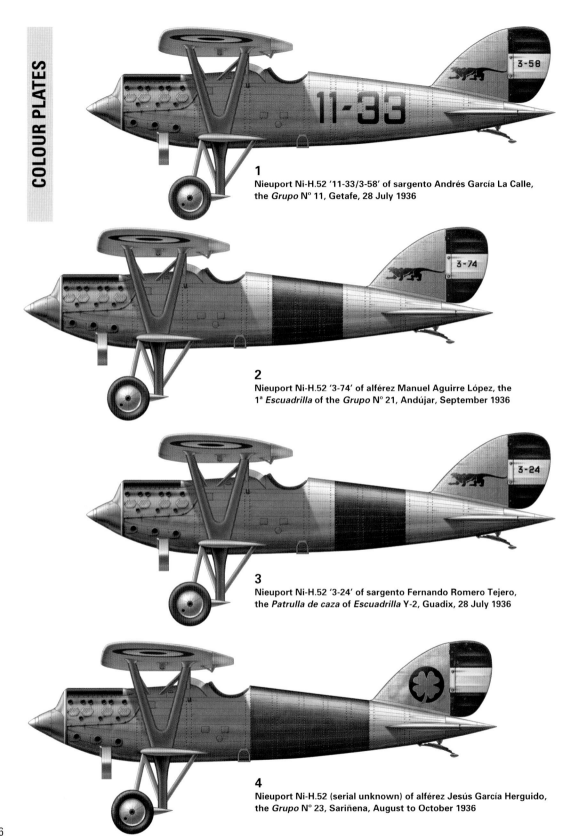

1
Nieuport Ni-H.52 '11-33/3-58' of sargento Andrés García La Calle,
the *Grupo* N° 11, Getafe, 28 July 1936

2
Nieuport Ni-H.52 '3-74' of alférez Manuel Aguirre López, the
1ª *Escuadrilla* of the *Grupo* N° 21, Andújar, September 1936

3
Nieuport Ni-H.52 '3-24' of sargento Fernando Romero Tejero,
the *Patrulla de caza* of *Escuadrilla* Y-2, Guadix, 28 July 1936

4
Nieuport Ni-H.52 (serial unknown) of alférez Jesús García Herguido,
the *Grupo* N° 23, Sariñena, August to October 1936

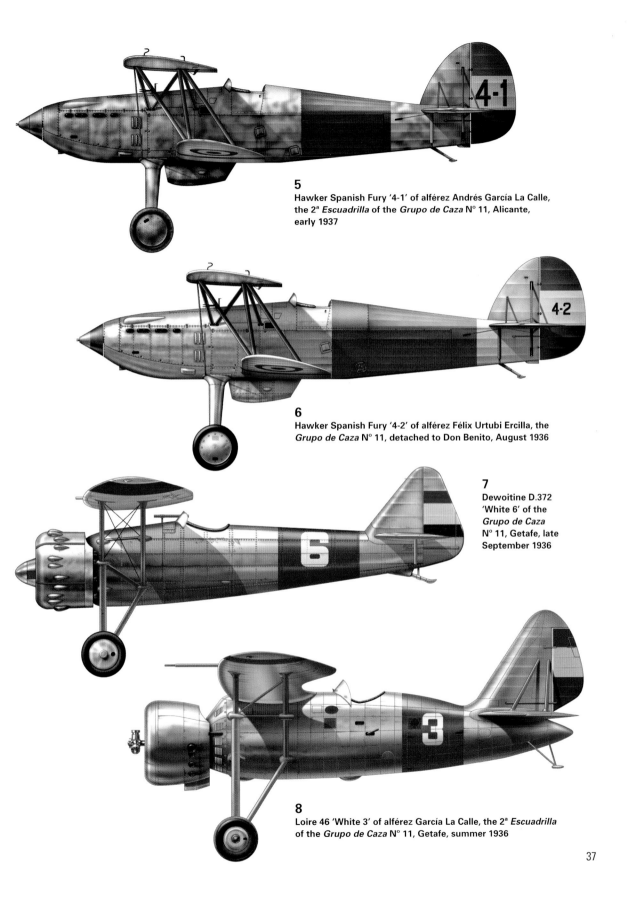

5
Hawker Spanish Fury '4-1' of alférez Andrés García La Calle, the 2ª *Escuadrilla* of the *Grupo de Caza* Nº 11, Alicante, early 1937

6
Hawker Spanish Fury '4-2' of alférez Félix Urtubi Ercilla, the *Grupo de Caza* Nº 11, detached to Don Benito, August 1936

7
Dewoitine D.372 'White 6' of the *Grupo de Caza* Nº 11, Getafe, late September 1936

8
Loire 46 'White 3' of alférez García La Calle, the 2ª *Escuadrilla* of the *Grupo de Caza* Nº 11, Getafe, summer 1936

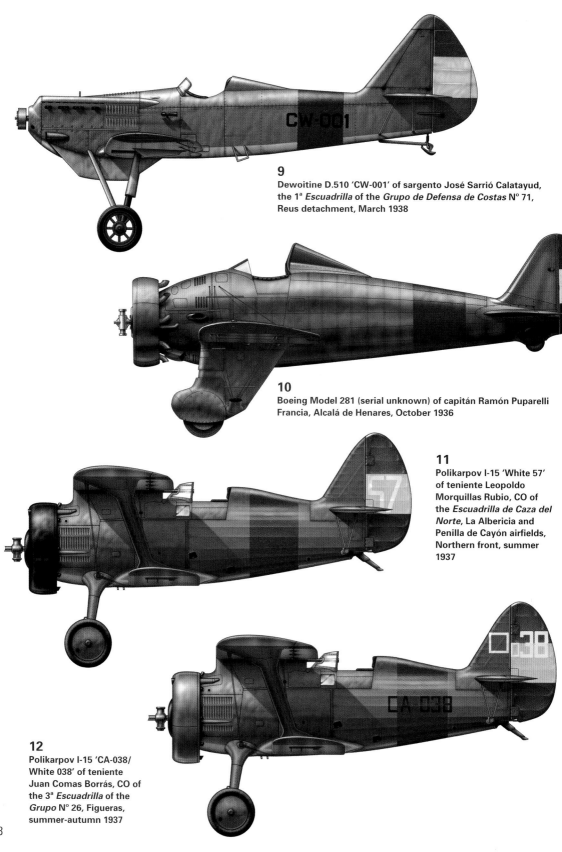

9
Dewoitine D.510 'CW-001' of sargento José Sarrió Calatayud, the 1ª *Escuadrilla* of the *Grupo de Defensa de Costas* Nº 71, Reus detachment, March 1938

10
Boeing Model 281 (serial unknown) of capitán Ramón Puparelli Francia, Alcalá de Henares, October 1936

11
Polikarpov I-15 'White 57' of teniente Leopoldo Morquillas Rubio, CO of the *Escuadrilla de Caza del Norte*, La Albericia and Penilla de Cayón airfields, Northern front, summer 1937

12
Polikarpov I-15 'CA-038/White 038' of teniente Juan Comas Borrás, CO of the 3ª *Escuadrilla* of the *Grupo* Nº 26, Figueras, summer-autumn 1937

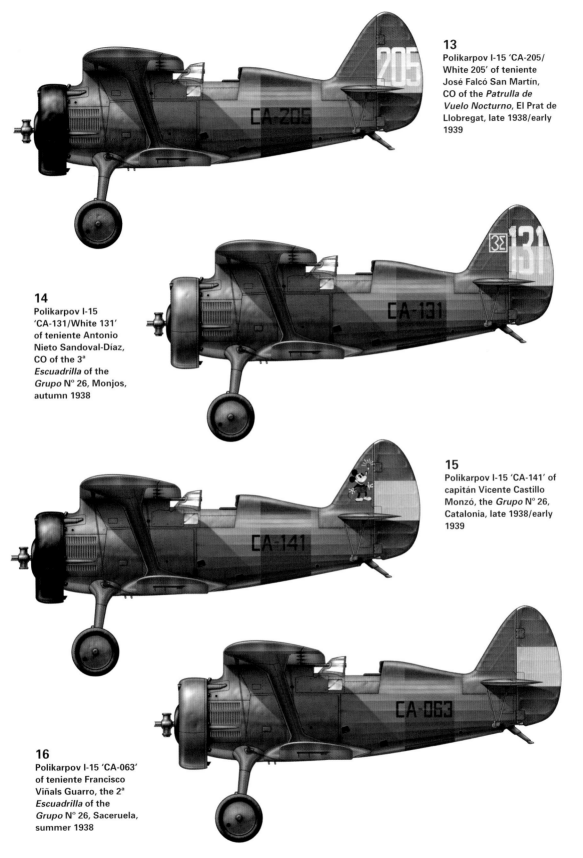

13
Polikarpov I-15 'CA-205/
White 205' of teniente
José Falcó San Martín,
CO of the *Patrulla de
Vuelo Nocturno*, El Prat de
Llobregat, late 1938/early
1939

14
Polikarpov I-15
'CA-131/White 131'
of teniente Antonio
Nieto Sandoval-Díaz,
CO of the 3ª
Escuadrilla of the
Grupo Nº 26, Monjos,
autumn 1938

15
Polikarpov I-15 'CA-141' of
capitán Vicente Castillo
Monzó, the *Grupo* Nº 26,
Catalonia, late 1938/early
1939

16
Polikarpov I-15 'CA-063'
of teniente Francisco
Viñals Guarro, the 2ª
Escuadrilla of the
Grupo Nº 26, Saceruela,
summer 1938

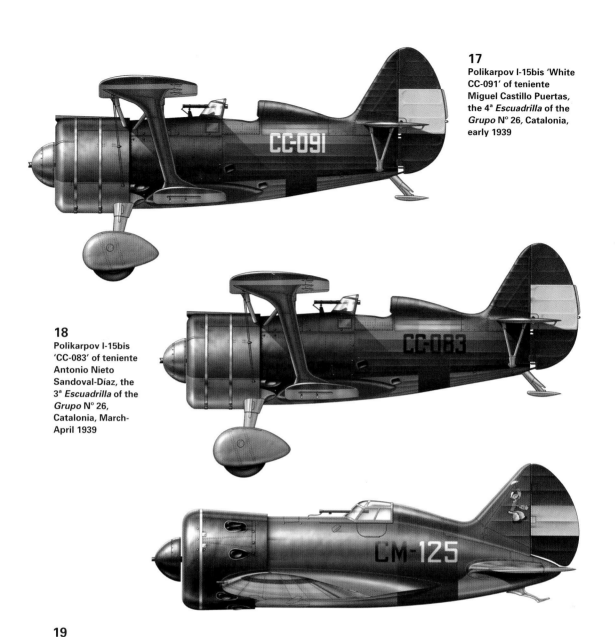

17
Polikarpov I-15bis 'White CC-091' of teniente Miguel Castillo Puertas, the 4ª *Escuadrilla* of the *Grupo* Nº 26, Catalonia, early 1939

18
Polikarpov I-15bis 'CC-083' of teniente Antonio Nieto Sandoval-Díaz, the 3ª *Escuadrilla* of the *Grupo* Nº 26, Catalonia, March-April 1939

19
Polikarpov I-16 Type 6 'CM-125' of capitán Manuel Zarauza Clavero, CO of the 4ª *Escuadrilla* of the *Grupo* Nº 21, Valencia, summer 1938

20
Polikarpov I-16 Type 10 'CM-157' of teniente Eduardo Claudín, CO of the 1ª *Escuadrilla* of the *Grupo* Nº 21, Liria, January 1938

21
Polikarpov I-16 Type 10 'CM-225' of mayor Manuel Zarauza Clavero, the *Grupo* N° 21 staff, Valencia, autumn 1938

22
Polikarpov I-16 Type 10 'CM-260' of teniente Antonio Arias Arias, CO of the 4ª *Escuadrilla* of the *Grupo* N° 21, El Vendrell, autumn 1938

23
Polikarpov I-16 Type 10 'CM-193' of teniente Francisco Tarazona Torán, CO of the 3ª *Escuadrilla* of the *Grupo* N° 21, Vilajuiga, February 1939

24
Polikarpov I-16 Type 10 'CM-249' of capitán José María Bravo Fernández of the *Grupo* N° 21, el Plá de Cabra, summer 1938

6
Hawker Spanish Fury '4-2' of alférez
Félix Urtubi Ercilla, the *Grupo de
Caza* Nº 11, detached to Don Benito,
August 1936

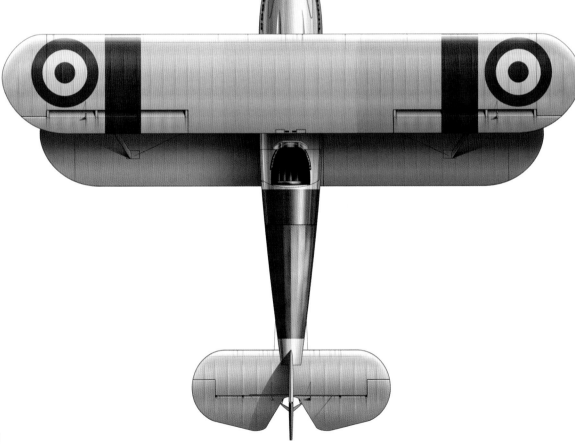

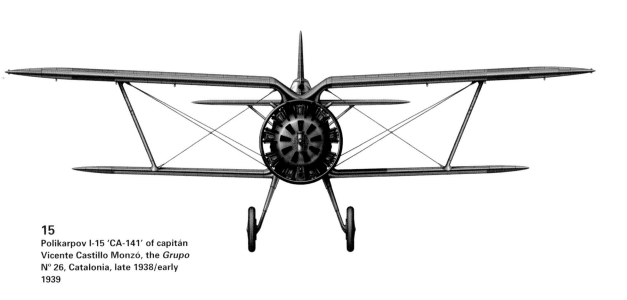

15
Polikarpov I-15 'CA-141' of capitán
Vicente Castillo Monzó, the *Grupo*
N° 26, Catalonia, late 1938/early
1939

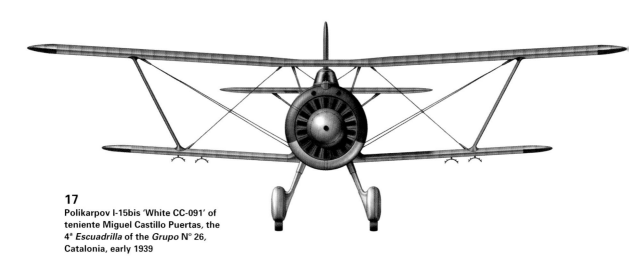

17
Polikarpov I-15bis 'White CC-091' of
teniente Miguel Castillo Puertas, the
4ª *Escuadrilla* of the *Grupo* N° 26,
Catalonia, early 1939

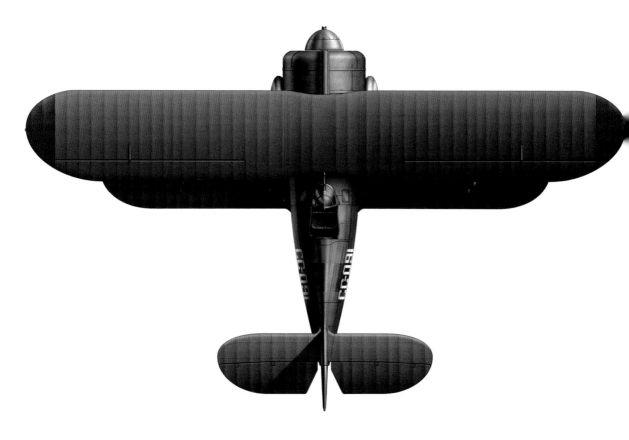

24
Polikarpov I-16 Type 10 'CM-249' of capitán José María Bravo Fernández of the *Grupo* Nº 21, el Plá de Cabra, summer 1938

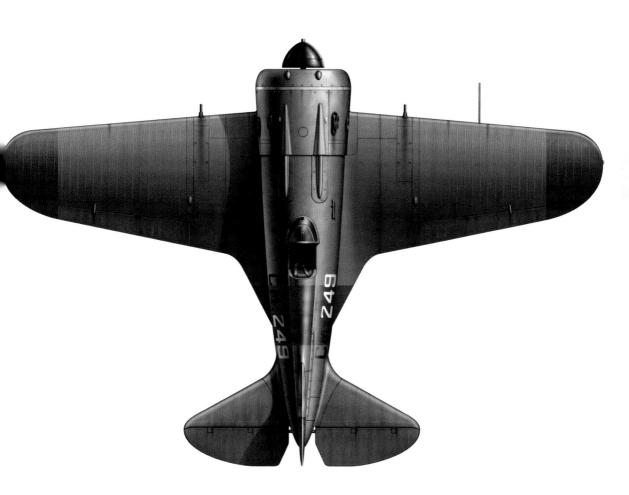

I-15 CHATO GRUPO Nº 26

The first 25 I-15s arrived in Spain in late October 1936, but their operational debut was far from successful. On 3 November two of these aircraft, and their Soviet pilots, landed by mistake in the province of Segovia and ended up in enemy hands. As it happened, these Soviet-built fighters were considered by the Nationalists to be merely copies of American Curtiss fighters, and this was how they continued to be regarded by the rebel forces. Yet over the following days the I-15s, popularly known to the Republicans as *Chatos,* made their presence felt during the defence of Madrid.

The Soviet command in Spain eventually permitted the best Spanish fighter pilots to join the two *escuadrillas* that had been established upon the I-15s' arrival. Aviators such as García La Calle, Fernando Roig Villalta and Augusto Martín Campos soon began flying the biplanes, and although the latter pilot was quickly dismissed because the Soviet command did not trust him, further Spanish pilots joined the *escuadrillas.* They included José Cuartero, Emilio Galera, Jesús García Herguido, Alfonso Jiménez Bruguet, Manuel Aguirre López, Roberto Alonso Santamaría and Rafael Robledano Ruiz.

The arrival of new aircraft from the Soviet Union, as well as the training of additional Spanish fighter pilots, permitted the establishment of the first Spanish I-15 *Chato escuadrilla* in February 1937. This unit's complement also included a number of American pilots under capitán Andrés García La Calle. A second *escuadrilla* was swiftly established under the command of capitán Roberto Alonso Santamaría. Finally, capitán Ramón Puparelli Francia was appointed as the first Spanish *Grupo de Caza* CO, his short-lived unit being designated the *Grupo* Nº 16. Both Spanish *escuadrillas* were to operate virtually independently, with one deployed to the Madrid front and the other to Aragon, before they were re-united during the battle of Guadalajara in March 1937.

The need for reinforcements in the north two months later saw the Spanish *escuadrillas* separated once again. The former *Escuadrilla La Calle*, now led by teniente José Riverola Grúas, arrived on the Northern front in two groups of six and ten aircraft on the 22nd and 24th, respectively.

During the battle of Brunete in July only one Spanish fighter unit was committed to the campaign –

An unidentified *Chato* pilot climbs into the cockpit of his fighter

the 2ª *Escuadrilla*, commanded by teniente Chindasvinto González García. Although the subsequent arrival of the first Spanish pilots trained in the USSR facilitated the establishment of new *escuadrillas*, reinforcements were again required on the Northern front, and this time they were led by capitán Puparelli.

The autumn of 1937 saw the establishment of the *Grupo* N⁰ 26, comprised of the Soviet 1ª *Escuadrilla* and the Spanish 2ª *Escuadrilla*. Both operated on the Aragon front. In October the 3ª *Escuadrilla* was formed at Figueras under the command of teniente Juan Comas Borrás, and by late November the core of the 4ª *Escuadrilla*, commanded by teniente Ladislao Duarte Espés, had also been gathered together from pilots and groundcrew evacuated from the north. This four *escuadrillas* structure was subsequently maintained by the *Grupo* N⁰ 26 for the rest of the war, as plans to create a 5ª *Escuadrilla* did not materialise. In the summer of 1938 capitán Chindasvinto González was appointed to lead the formerly Soviet 1ª *Escuadrilla*, and he was soon succeeded by teniente Vicente Castillo Monzó.

The I-15 *Chato* was regarded as a jack-of-all-trades by the Republicans, these versatile, fast and manoeuvrable biplanes being entrusted with many different missions, including bomber escort, frontline patrolling, strafing, light bombing (some were fitted with bomb racks) and nightfighting. *Chatos* were also constructed under licence in Spain, with production of 300 aircraft being planned but only 213 built. Many were delivered to operational units and the rest were captured as incomplete airframes by the victorious Nationalists. A final batch of I-15bis *Superchato* fighters, which had more powerful engines that made them both heavier and faster, as well as wheel-spats and a flat upper wing, arrived during the final months of the campaign in Catalonia. They had virtually no effect on the outcome of the conflict, however, these machines ending up in France after their pilots fled to Carcasonne on 6 March 1939.

The only group decoration awarded to the Republican *Fuerzas Aéreas* was the *Distintivo al Valor* (Ensign of Valour), which went to the 1ª *Escuadrilla* of *Grupo* N⁰ 26 for its strafing missions flown during operations in Catalonia. The award was gazetted on 16 January 1939 in the *Diario Oficial del Ministerio de Defensa Nacional* N⁰ 16.

Spanish COs of the *Grupo* N⁰ 16 *Chato escuadrillas*

Grupo de Caza N⁰ 16
Andrés García La Calle
Roberto Alonso Santamaría
Javier Jover Rovira
Alfonso Jiménez Bruguet
José Riverola Grúas

Grupo N⁰ 26
Ramón Puparelli Francia
Juan Armario Álvarez
Miguel Zambudio Martínez
Vicente Castillo Monzó
Ladislao Duarte Espés

1ª *Escuadrilla*
Chindasvinto González García
Gerardo Gil Sánchez
Vicente Castillo Monzó
Jaime Torn Roca

2ª *Escuadrilla*
Chindasvinto González García
Gerardo Gil Sánchez
Leopoldo Morquillas Rubio
Francisco Viñals Guarro

3ª *Escuadrilla*
Juan Comas Borrás
Miguel Zambudio Martínez
Antonio Nieto Sandoval Díaz
Álvaro Muñoz López

4ª *Escuadrilla*
Ladislao Duarte Espés
Emilio Ramírez Bravo
Miguel Castillo Puertas

Juan José Armario Álvarez

Born at Jerez de la Frontera, in Cádiz, on 20 November 1906, Juan José Armario Álvarez joined the flying course at the *Escuela de Aeronáutica Naval* in Barcelona in 1923. At El Prat de Llobregat airfield he flew Avro 504K biplanes under the guidance of his British instructor, Harry Brown. Graduating as a land-based pilot, Armario undertook the flying boat course on Macchi M.18s at the Contradique base, in Barcelona. During his training he also flew Martinsyde F 4 Buzzard fighters and Savoia S.62 flying boats.

When the *Cuerpo Auxiliar de Aeronáutica Naval* was established by the new Republic, Armario became one of its first officers. After success in a demanding examination he was appointed oficial segundo (sub-lieutenant) and posted to the *Escuela de Aeronáutica* in Barcelona. Here he flew CASA E-30, Dornier Wal and Vickers Vildebeest aircraft, as well as L.A.P.E. Fokker F.VII/3m tri-motors in order to gain a commercial pilot's licence.

At the time of the military uprising in July 1936, Juan José Armario was a flying instructor at the *Escuadrilla Escuela de la Aeronáutica Naval* in Barcelona. Flying his first operational sortie on 20 July 1936, he bombed the Atarazanas barracks while flying an S.62. Armario also logged reconnaissance missions over the River Ebro up to Saragossa. Continuing to fly the S.62, he participated in the August landing operations on Majorca that were led by capitán Alberto Bayo of the *Aviación Militar*. Armario returned to Barcelona after a large number of government seaplanes were lost to Italian-flown Savoia S.55s, Macchi M.41s and land-based CR.32s.

On 1 December a decision was taken to move the *Escuela de Hidros* from Barcelona to the *Base Aeronaval* at San Javier. Capitán Armario was

Capitán Juan José Armario Álvarez of the *Aeronáutica Naval* took command of I-15-equipped *Grupo* N° 26 after leading night-bombing *Grupo* N° 11 followed by the *Escuela de Hidros* (Seaplane School). He flew as a formation leader during the well-known strafing attack on Garrapinillos airfield, in Zaragoza, on 15 October 1937, which saw a dozen enemy aircraft destroyed

appointed CO of the new base, arriving on the 21st. It was to be a brief posting, for in February 1937 he was made commander of the night-bombing unit *Grupo Mixto* N° 11. This unit consisted of one *escuadrilla* equipped with Fokker F.VII/3m, F.XII and F.XVIII tri-motors and another operating twin-engined Potez 54, Breguet Vultur and Marcel Bloch 210 aircraft. It was based initially at Los Alcázares, but later moved to Lérida airfield. While leading this unit Armario flew night bombing sorties on the Huesca and Saragossa fronts, as well as liaison flights to the north.

On 9 October 1937 he was appointed CO of I-15 *Grupo* N° 26, which initially comprised three *escuadrillas* with 15 aircraft each. The 1ª *Escuadrilla* was led by Soviet ace Evgeniy Nikolaevich Stepanov, while teniente Gerardo Gil headed up the 2ª *Escuadrilla* and teniente Juan Comas Borrás commanded the 3ª *Escuadrilla*. A 4ª *Escuadrilla* was formed soon afterwards under teniente Ladislao Duarte.

Armario initially flew with the Soviet *patrulla* of the staff flight of the *Grupo* N° 26, often accompanying Stepanov. During a night flight on 19 October this *patrulla* downed a SIAI SM.81 tri-motor over Barcelona, the bomber crashing in flames in Republican territory near Sabadell.

Armario's most noteworthy action in the campaign had come four days earlier when he led a strafing attack on Garrapinillos airfield, in Saragossa. To ensure the success of this raid, the armourers worked through the night loading the aircrafts' machine guns with incendiary ammunition. The *Chatos* of the 1ª and 2ª *Escuadrillas*, led by capitán Armario himself, carried out the attack on the parked aircraft, while the I-16 *grupo* flew top cover. According to pilots' reports, no fewer than 26 aircraft (both fighters and bombers) were destroyed, although the actual figure was lower.

On 9 February 1938, at the height of the battle of Teruel, Armario was promoted to mayor de Aviación Naval on the basis of his war record and confirmed as CO of the *Grupo de Chatos* N° 26 on 25 February. Mayor Armario continued to command the unit through the various campaigns in Aragon, Levante and the Ebro, often leading his *escuadrillas* personally. On 24 September, during the battle of the Ebro, he departed the *Grupo* N° 26 to join the *Jefe de Estado Mayor de Fuerzas Aéreas* in Barcelona. For a time Armario was attached to the headquarters of the *Ejército del Ebro* as an aviation adviser to the commander of the army, coronel Modesto. His last posting came on 28 October 1938 when he was appointed *Jefe de la 3ª Sección* (Operations) of the *Estado Mayor de las Fuerzas Aéreas de la Zona Norte* (Barcelona).

Armario fled to France after the fall of Catalonia and was interned there. He subsequently moved to Mexico and died in Mexico City on 8 February 1990.

Juan Comas Borrás

Having been born at Lloret de Mar, in Gerona, on 31 January 1913, Juan Comas Borrás was just 15 when he enrolled in the *Escuela de Aeronáutica*

Naval in Barcelona. On completing the courses there he moved to the *Escuela Civil de Pilotos* in Albacete. Comas flew the school's Avro 504K and Bristol F 2B biplane trainers, and subsequently graduated as a Piloto Aviador. He then returned to the *Escuela de Hidros* in Barcelona to take a seaplane course at the Contradique quay, after which he flew Macchi M.18s. In 1932 Comas applied for a discharge from the *Aeronáutica Naval* on family grounds.

At the start of the civil war Comas joined the *Aeronáutica Naval* in Barcelona, and in September he was sent to the *Escuela de Pilotos* at San Javier for a refresher course. Requesting reinstatement in his original service, Comas was subsequently accepted as a maestre of the *Aeronáutica Naval* in November 1936. In late February 1937 he was posted to the I-15-equipped 2ª *Escuadrilla*, commanded by capitán Roberto Alonso Santamaría, for operations on the Aragon front from the airfields at Lérida, Castejón del Puente and Sarrión (Teruel). On 17 April Comas participated in a fierce battle between 15 *Chatos* and three He 51 *escuadrillas*. He damaged the enemy biplane flown by alférez Javier Allende but chivalrously escorted it until the pilot was able to make a forced-landing in Nationalist-held territory.

On 17 May the unit attempted to fly north via France, with mayor Antonio Martín Luna-Lersundi leading in a DC-2. The formation crossed the Pyrenees in a snowstorm, but despite poor visibility Comas stuck to the DC-2's tail, followed by the other I-15 fighter pilots. However, the *patrulla* comprising teniente Ángel Cristiá and sargentos Manuel Zarauza and José Marín had to return to Lérida. The remaining I-15 pilots, meanwhile, landed safely at Pont-Long airfield, in Pau, and two days later they were allowed to return to Spain.

The *escuadrilla*, now led by teniente José Riverola, tried to reach Santander again on 24 May, but the only *patrulla* that managed to land at La Albericia airfield was comprised of Comas, Alarcón and Palomar. Sargento Zarauza turned back with engine trouble just after crossing the Sierra in Madrid, while teniente José Bastida ditched off San Sebastián and was captured. The other aircraft, led by Riverola, landed at Sondica.

Portrait of capitán Juan Comas Borrás, CO of the 3ª *Escuadrilla* and, subsequently, I-15 *Chato*-equipped *Grupo* Nº 26

Capitán Juan Comas Borrás poses in the cockpit of his I-15

In early August Comas left for Valencia by DC-2 for a spell of leave, returning to the north on the 17th with three *Chatos*. He was immediately appointed CO of the new 3ª *Escuadrilla* of the *Grupo* Nº 26, which had been established in the central area at Figueras airfield. On 18 August he became a teniente, with fellow pilots Ladislao Duarte, Miguel Zambudio Martinez, José Rodríguez Panadero and José Redondo Martín also being promoted. In October the unit was operating from Reus airfield, but in November it moved to Barracas, in Valencia, in preparation for the battle of Teruel. On 28 December teniente Comas claimed to have downed two CR.32s, and two days later he shot down a Bf 109. The destruction of a second Messerschmitt fighter was credited to him on 20 January 1938.

In March 1938 Comas was promoted to capitán for his conduct during the battle of Teruel, as were other distinguished *escuadrilla* COs Duarte, Morquillas, Claudín and Zarauza. After further leave, Comas was injured in a landing accident at El Toro airfield on 15 May when the undercarriage of his *Chato* collapsed, resulting in him spending several months in hospital at Torrente, in Valencia. Fully recovered by 22 September, Comas assumed command of the *Grupo* Nº 26 at Valls airfield. He had been preceded in this appointment by capitanes Ramón Puparelli and Juan José Armario. On that same day, whilst flying *Chato* 'CA-190' of the *grupo* staff, he was forced to land at Reus. Comas

Juan Comas Borrás, wearing French-made flying gear (popular with Republican pilots), enjoys a cigarette between sorties

Pilots of the 3ª *Escuadrilla de Chatos* of the *Grupo de Caza* Nº 26 at La Señera airfield in March 1938. Standing, from left to right, are José Falcó San Martín, José Redondo Martín, Benigno Domingo Huesco, CO teniente Juan Comas Borrás, Fulgencio Martínez Montoya, Antonio Britz Martínez, Antonio Sánchez, Miguel Zambudio Martínez and Cayetano Ortega Frías. Squatting, from left to right, are teniente Elías Hernández Camisón, Antonio Nieto Sandoval-Díaz, Jesús Pérez Pérez and Francisco Montagut Ferrer

Another group shot of pilots from the 3ª *Escuadrilla de Chatos* of the *Grupo de Caza* Nº 26 at La Señera airfield in March 1938. They are, from left to right, Elías Hernández Camisón, Benigno Domingo Huesco, José Falcó San Martín, Jacinto Puig Bastóns, Antonio Nieto Sandoval-Díaz, Antonio Sánchez, Francisco Montagut Ferrer, Antonio Britz Martínez, Jesús Pérez Pérez, Cayetano Ortega Frías, José Redondo Martín, Miguel Zambudio Martínez and CO teniente Juan Comas Borrás

subsequently moved with the staff flight to airfields at Sabadell and Monjos, in Barcelona, from where he flew sorties over the Ebro front in October in *Chato* 'CA-166'.

While based at Monjos airfield Comas received serious shrapnel wounds in his left leg during a raid by Savoia-Marchetti SM.79s on 5 November. Comas was taken to hospital at Villafranca de Penedés, where his leg was amputated. Whilst recuperating he was promoted to mayor de Aviación. On 7 February 1939, at the end of the campaign in Catalonia, Comas escaped from the Clínica Platón in Barcelona to France by ambulance. He remained hospitalised for a further six months, and was subsequently interned at Gurs. After the German occupation of France he was handed over to the Spanish authorities and court-martialled. Upon his release from prison, Comas settled at Tordera, in Barcelona, and he became its mayor during the 1980s.

Juan Comas Borrás died on 2 May 1992. He had distinguished himself during the civil war as one of the most experienced I-15 pilots, logging more than 500 sorties with the *Chato* and scoring seven confirmed and several probable victories.

José Riverola Grúas

Born in Grau, Huesca, on 27 August 1905, José Riverola Grúas joined the *Servicio de Aviación*, at the *Escuela de Mecánicos*, at Cuatro Vientos on 20 August 1925. He graduated in March 1927 and was promoted to cabo mecánico in September 1929. When the civil war broke out Riverola was posted to the Wal-equipped *Grupo de Hidros* Nº 6 at Los Alcázares airfield, in Murcia. Having logged many flying hours, he was promoted to sargento mecánico and took a pilot's course at La Ribera. He graduated in October 1936 and soon afterwards trained as a fighter pilot.

In February 1937, shortly before the end of the battle of the Jarama, Riverola was posted to the I-15 *Chato escuadrilla* commanded by capitán Andrés García La Calle. He participated in the battle of Guadalajara and led the 12 *Chatos* that flew north on 24 May. Flying I-15 '83' in company with six other pilots, Riverola landed at Sondica, with further fighters making it to La Albericia.

As CO of the *Escuadrilla de Caza del Norte*, Riverola took part in the final phase of the Biscay campaign in May-June 1937, but lost most of his aircraft in frequent air raids on Somorrostro airfield. In July, after the arrival of a new *Chato* element led by the *Grupo* Nº 26 CO capitán Ramón Puparelli, Riverola returned to the central area. Promoted to capitán on 30 June 1937, he joined the *Escuela de Caza* and was subsequently ordered to form the 3ª *Escuadrilla* of *Grupo* Nº 26 at Manises airfield in Valencia. The unit was later transferred to Rosas (Gerona) and Sabadell. On 24 August Riverola shot down an SM.81 tri-motor over the Gulf of Rosas.

In September 1937 he was interim commander of the *Grupo* Nº 26, but on the 26th of that month Riverola was appointed CO of the fighter units assigned to the *Escuadra Mixta* Nº 7 *de protección de costas* (Mixed Coastal Wing Nº 7), equipped with Dewoitine D.371/372s, Dewoitine D.510s, captured CR.32s and Gourdou Leseurre GL.32s. On 1 December Riverola was also appointed aviation liaison officer on the staff of the auxiliary *Base Naval* at Rosas.

Tenientes José Riverola and Gerardo Gil. The former replaced García La Calle as CO of the *Escuadrilla La Calle* just prior to it being sent to the Northern front in May 1937

On 5 May 1938 Riverola became deputy CO of the new *Grupo de Asalto* N° 28, which was equipped with Grumman GE-23 *Delfín* aircraft and based at Cardedeu airfield. On 30 June he was transferred to Valencia with the 1ª *Escuadrilla* of the *grupo* to fly defensive patrols over the port. The unit also operated from Alcantarilla, El Carmolí, Los Alcázares and La Aparecida airfields in Murcia. During the summer of 1938 Riverola's Grummans were briefly committed to the Extremadura fronts, based at Saceruela and Almodóvar del Campo airfields.

From October 1938 capitán Riverola assumed command of *Grupo* N° 71 of the *Zona Aérea Centro-Sur*. This unit, consisting of two squadrons (namely the mixed 4ª *Escuadrilla* and the 5ª *Escuadrilla* operating bombers only), took part in the defence of the Cartagena area. With the end of the war Riverola flew into exile in Algeria, leading a mixed *Chato* and *Delfín* formation to Oran. No further information is available on him.

Leopoldo Morquillas Rubio

Leopoldo Morquillas Rubio was born in 1915 into a family with a military background. In early 1933, at the age of 18, he joined the air force as a private and was posted to the *Escuadra* N° 3, based at El Prat de Llobregat airfield. Promoted to cabo, he was subsequently transferred to Logroño airfield. At the outbreak of hostilities Morquillas was on leave in Madrid, but he volunteered for duty at Getafe airfield.

The shortage of flying personnel prompted him to apply for a commission as an air gunner-bombardier, and he duly flew sorties in Breguet 19s and Potez 540s over the sierra and to the outskirts of Madrid. During this period Morquillas flew with pilots Arcega, Areán, Cremades, Cascón, Jiménez, Hortelano, Lurueña, Peña, Ramos, Ricote, Salvoch and Valls. He was shot down three times, twice while flying Breguet 19s and once in a Potez 540. On the third occasion, on 28 October 1936, he and sargento piloto Vicente Valls Bort fell victim to CR.32s, but they managed to force land in a field. Both men were unhurt.

In November Morquillas enrolled in the *Escuela de Pilotos* at La Ribera, where he trained alongside Zarauza, Comas, Zambudio, Magriñá and Rodríguez Panadero. Morquillas graduated as a pilot on 3 February 1937, and later that month flew Ni-H.52s (he was assigned '3-25') with the *patrulla de protección* (duty flight) at Reus airfield together with teniente Luis Tuya and sargento Miguel Zambudio. In March 1937 he was transferred to the Northern front, being flown to Santander in a DC-2. Promoted to the rank of teniente on 22 March, Morquillas flew Š-231s and GL.32s, as well as I-15 *Chatos* attached to the Soviet *escuadrilla* that was commanded by the Soviet pilot Baranchuk. Having claimed a He 51 on 17 April for his first aerial victory, Morquillas subsequently served under teniente

Pilots of the 1ª and 2ª *Escuadrilla de Chatos* of the *Grupo de Caza* N° 26 at Alcublas airfield, in Valencia, in 1938. Standing, from left to right, are Antonio Aguilar Ambrosio (2ª), Juan Lloréns Bonet (2ª), Melchor Diaz Román (1ª), Felipe Cirujeda Esteve (1ª), Francisco Viñals Guarro (2ª), Leopoldo Morquillas Rubio (2ª *Escuadrilla* CO), Julián Barbero López (2ª *Escuadrilla* deputy CO) and Antonio Janoher Buendía (1ª). Squatting, from left to right, are Juan Andreu Motes (2ª), Vicente Baixaulí Soria (2ª), Joaquín Calvo Diago (2ª), José Brufau Basanta (2ª), Francisco Sagasti Fernández (2ª), José Mora *Fauría* (2ª) and Juan Sayós Estivill (1ª)

Felipe del Río and then teniente Baquedano Moreno on the Biscay and Santander fronts. When these two pilots were shot down, teniente Riverola assumed command, and on his transfer to the Central front teniente Morquillas was appointed CO of the *Escuadrilla de Caza del Norte*. By that time he was flying *Chato* 'CA-57' from La Albericia and Penilla de Cayón airfields, in Santander.

Leopoldo Morquillas' I-15, which has been adorned with a triangle marking on the tail to denote its assignment to the CO of the *2ª Escuadrilla*

In August 1937, a few days before the fall of Santander, an exhausted Morquillas was flown out by DC-2 to Barcelona, where he assumed command of the unit defending the city from El Prat de Llobregat airfield. Subsequently posted to the 3ª *Escuadrilla de Chatos* as deputy CO, Morquillas was given command of the 2ª *Escuadrilla*, based at Villar airfield, in Valencia, on 11 January 1938. There, he operated over the Teruel front and made a number of claims. On 17 January he reported shooting down a CR.32, followed by another the next day. He claimed a CR.32 damaged on the 20th and another Fiat fighter as a probable on 21 February.

Morquillas continued to lead the 2ª *Escuadrilla de Chatos* on the Aragon and Levante fronts, and was promoted to capitán on 7 March. In June he was selected to head up a group of four I-15 pilots, one I-16 pilot and two SB pilots that were to be sent to the USSR for training at the Tactical High School in Lipetsk. The aviators sailed for the USSR on 23 August, and while there Leopoldo Morquillas was promoted to mayor. Because of the length of the course the group was still in the Soviet Union when the Spanish conflict ended in late March 1939.

Remaining in the USSR, the Spanish pilots became flying and combat instructors at Soviet schools in 1941, but subsequently flew as ground attack and fighter unit commanders on the Eastern Front. Morquillas, who led an assault *eskadrilya* and was subsequently made inspector of an air division, served in the Soviet air force for ten years and was awarded numerous decorations during that time. Retiring in 1948, he became a factory manager at Tula, where he married and settled down. Morquillas died in the USSR some years ago.

Miguel Zambudio Martínez

Born on 2 September 1918 at Puente Tocinos, in Murcia, Miguel Zambudio Martínez joined the Republican air force in September 1936. He enrolled in the pilot's course at the *Escuela de Vuelo y Combate* at Alcalá de Henares, from where he moved to Santiago de la Ribera for elementary and fighter pilot training. By this time Zambudio had already flown the DH 60 Moth Major, Hispano-Suiza E-34, Breguet 19, Miles Hawk, Caudron C.600 Aiglon, Fleet 10, Morane-Saulnier MS.230, GL.32, Koolhoven FK.51, Avro 626 and Ni-H.52.

On completion of the fighter course on 11 February 1937, Zambudio was sent to Reus to fly Ni-H.52 '3-15'. According to base CO capitán Manuel Gayoso, he quickly damaged three Nieuport fighters and retraining was recommended. Despite this inauspicious start, Zambudio ultimately proved to be a talented pilot and was posted to the Northern front on 23 March. He arrived there with a group of fighter pilots on board a DC-2. At Bilbao, sargento Zambudio was posted to a new *escuadrilla* equipped with the Š.231, which was found to be unsuitable for combat with modern German fighters. Shortly thereafter he was assigned to fly further obsolete equipment in the shape of French GL.32 parasol fighters, which had arrived in the north without armament. Hastily fitted with two bomb racks on the wing struts, they were pressed into service as light bombers. On 30 April Zambudio took off from La Albericia airfield at the controls

A close-up of teniente Miguel Zambudio Martínez sitting in the cockpit of his I-15 on alert while he was CO of the 3ª *Escuadrilla*. Notice the small side windows that afforded some view forward from the cockpit on takeoff and landing and the huge gunsight

Parked on rocky ground in his I-15, Miguel Zambudio Martínez scans the skies for signs of enemy aircraft

of one of these extemporised bombers to attack the Nationalist battleship *España*, which had hit a mine and was already sinking.

Zambudio later joined the *Escuadrilla de Caza del Norte* and flew *Chatos* in the Biscay, Santander and Asturias campaigns. In August he claimed his first success when he was credited with the destruction of a Bf 109. On 2 September Zambudio's aircraft was set on fire in combat with German fighters after his mixed formation of I-15s and I-16s was attacked while supporting government forces over Llanes. Although he managed to bail out, Zambudio landed in no-man's-land. Despite having been lightly wounded, he escaped and reached friendly lines. Zambudio, who was soon flying again, was promoted to teniente before the end of the fighting in the north. The situation in Gijón was critical when, on

Pilots of the 3ª *Escuadrilla* of the *Grupo de Caza* Nº 26 in 1938. Miguel Zambudio is standing closest to the camera in the white overalls. To his right is teniente Antonio Nieto

20 October, he and other pilots and groundcrew fled for neighbouring France, thus bringing the ill-fated campaign in the north to an end.

Moving to Catalonia, Zambudio was posted to the 3ª *Escuadrilla de Chatos*, which was being established at Figueras airfield under the command of teniente Juan Comas. During an engagement on the Aragon front on 10 December, teniente Zambudio claimed a share in the destruction of a *Legion Condor* He 111. Now based at El Toro, the 3ª *Escuadrilla*, together with teniente Morquillas' 2ª *Escuadrilla*, took part in operations over Teruel. It also

helped cover the retreat from Aragon in March 1938, flying from Caspe and Bujaraloz.

When teniente José Redondo was sent on a *Mosca* course at the *Escuela de Alta Velocidad* at El Carmolí, Zambudio was appointed CO of the 3ª *Escuadrilla de Chatos*. He led the unit during operations over Levante in May and June and also in the Ebro offensive. Zambudio was promoted to capitán on 1 October, and the following month he was appointed CO of the *Grupo* Nº 26 in succession to Comas, who had suffered leg wounds during an air raid on Monjos airfield. On 24 December, during the enemy offensive in Catalonia, Zambudio was leading *Grupo* Nº 26 on a sortie over the Serós bridgehead when his unit was attacked by Bf 109s and CR.32s. He sustained leg wounds, including damage to the sciatic nerve, in the ensuing melée and was admitted to hospital in Barcelona. Zambudio was subsequently evacuated to Camprodón, from where he escaped to France and internment, in company with Comas, following the Republican surrender.

Zambudio settled in France post-war and became a businessman. Eventually returning to Spain, he passed away in December 1996.

Vicente Castillo Monzó

Vicente Castillo Monzó was born in Benaguacil, Valencia, on 29 January 1917. In December 1936 he joined the *Arma de Aviación*, enrolling in the elementary flying course at La Ribera airfield. On 17 January 1937 he sailed on the SS *Ciudad de Cádiz* for the USSR, where he joined a pilots' course at Kirovabad. Returning to Spain in June, Castillo received his pilot's badge and the rank of sargento. On 8 July he joined the I-15-equipped 2ª *Escuadrilla* of the *Grupo* Nº 26 at Archena airfield, in Murcia. As a member of this unit he moved to Chozas de la Sierra and took part in air combat over Brunete. On 18 July Castillo fought in his first aerial battle and claimed a He 51 destroyed. The unit was subsequently transferred to Azuqueca de Henares and, on 23 August, to Alcañiz, in Saragossa.

It was from the latter airfield that Castillo participated in a series of combats over Belchite and claimed a number of aerial victories. Between 24 and 26 August he downed two CR.32s over Leciñena and Perdiguera, a third over Fuentes de Ebro and a Meridionali Ro.37 over Caspe. The *escuadrilla* operated from Sariñena during the battles that took place in the early days of September, Castillo shooting down two more CR.32s over Escatrón on the 2nd. The 2ª *Escuadrilla* then moved to the airfield at Candasnos to take part in operations over Fuentes de Ebro. On 15 October sargento Castillo participated in the highly successful strafing attack on Garrapinillos airfield, and on 10 December he claimed to have shot down a Nationalist CR.32. On the 26th the

A close-up of capitán Vicente Castillo Monzó posing alongside the tail of I-15 'CA-141' of the 1ª *Escuadrilla* of the *Grupo* Nº 26 in Catalonia in late 1938/early 1939. Monzó, the last CO of the *Grupo* Nº 26, adopted Disney's popular 'Mickey Mouse' cartoon character as his personal emblem. The ace is wearing a long leather flying jacket in this photograph

Pilots of the 1ª *Escuadrilla de Chatos* of the *Grupo de Caza* Nº 26 in 1938. They are, from left to right, Francisco Janoher Buendía, Vicente Pradiés Victoria, Juan Sayós Estivill, Manuel Arasa Sabaté, unidentified, Vicente Castillo Monzó (*escuadrilla* CO), Basilio Fernández-Grande Luengo, Melchor Díaz Román, Alberto Vallés Gateu and an unidentified pilot squatting at the front

2ª *Escuadrilla* was transferred to El Toro airfield in the 4ª *Región Aérea* to participate in operations over Teruel.

Castillo, who had been promoted to teniente in February 1938, moved with the 2ª *Escuadrilla* to Requena airfield, Valencia, following the completion of operations over Teruel – it remained here until 30 June 1938. In July Vicente Castillo was appointed CO of 1ª *Escuadrilla* of the *Grupo* Nº 26 in succession to capitán Chindasvinto González, and he marked his promotion by downing a CR.32 between Altura and Cueva Santa during operations over Levante in July. Later in the month the 1ª *Escuadrilla* was transferred to Valls airfield, before moving to Sabanell in early August. In subsequent operations over the Ebro during September teniente Castillo downed a Bf 109, which crashed in government-held territory, and a CR.32. In November, having been promoted to capitán, Castillo was credited with his final two successes when he claimed two CR.32s destroyed over the Segre area.

A well-known photograph of capitán Castillo Monzó's I-15 'CA-141' of the 1ª *Escuadrilla, Grupo* Nº 26 being refuelled prior to flying its next sortie

In December he was appointed CO of the *Grupo de Chatos* Nº 26, succeeding capitán Miguel Zambudio, who had been wounded in combat. January 1939 saw capitán Castillo and his unit transferred to Sisones airfield, in the Central-Southern area, to participate in operations over Extremadura. The *Grupo de Chatos* Nº 26 later left for Manises, where it remained until being transferred to La Rabasa airfield on 29 March. Here, its aircraft were reluctantly surrendered to Nationalist forces after groundcrew refused to refuel them. Initially confined in Santa Bárbara castle, Castillo was court-martialled at Valencia and sentenced to death. The sentence was eventually commuted to life in prison, but he was released under an amnesty in June 1943.

The third-ranking Spanish ace of the Republican air arm with 13 victories, Vicente Castillo had logged 550 hours and flown

350 operational sorties during the war (mostly in the I-15 *Chato*). Castillo died in Barcelona on 16 June 1981.

Chindasvinto González García

Born at Urda, in Toledo, on 11 March 1911, Chindasvinto González García joined the *Servicio de Aviación* at the *Escuela de Mecánicos* at Cuatro Vientos in February 1930. He graduated as a mechanic in June 1932 and was posted to *Escuadrilla* Y-2 at the *Escuela de Tiro y Bombardeo* at Los Alcázares airfield. A further posting followed in November 1934 to the *Escuela de Vuelo y Combate* at Alcalá de Henares. González was subsequently appointed flight engineer on Fokker F.VII/3m '20-4' and then underwent training on multi-engined aircraft.

The start of the civil war caught González on leave in Madrid, and he joined his unit on 18 July. Ten days later he was posted to Getafe airfield, from where he operated as a sargento mecánico with the *Escuadrilla Mixta de Breguet XIX y Nieuport 52* led by capitán Juan Quintana Ladrón de Guevara. The unit moved first to Don Benito airfield and then to Herrera del Duque for operations on the Extremadura front. González was promoted to sargento mecánico in August 1936. Returning to Getafe in late September, he served as a flight engineer for the DH 89 Dragon Rapide flown by teniente Miguel Kiriguine – a White Russian whose name has also been rendered in Spanish records as 'Kriguine', 'Kryguine' and 'Kringuin'. González flew with Kiriguine on liaison missions between Los Alcázares and Alcalá de Henares.

In early December González joined the *Escuela de Vuelos* pilots' course at San Javier in December 1936 as a brigada mecánico. At the school he logged only four hours of dual training on DH 60 Moth Majors, but flew 14 hours solo and 17 hours on Breguet 19s. In January 1937 González completed his basic flying training, after which he took the fighter pilots' course. He logged 11 hours that month, and a further 12 hours on Ni-H.52s in February. The school CO, comandante Félix Sampil, rated González as 'highly skilled, devoted and particularly suitable for fighter operations'. After completing the course, however, he was posted not to a fighter unit but to the 1ª *Escuadrilla* of the *Grupo* Nº 20, equipped with Polikarpov R-Z *Natacha* light bombers and commanded by capitán Crescencio Ramos. This unit operated from the airfields at Albacete, Tembleque, Linares and Madridejos.

In March 1937 González was promoted to teniente piloto, the alférez and brigada ranks having by then been abolished. On 20 April his aircraft was damaged during a battle with CR.32s on the Andalusian front, his gunner/bombardier, sargento Florentino Jiménez de la Fuente, being killed by enemy fire. In early May teniente González was posted to the 1ª *Escuadrilla* of the *Natacha Grupo* Nº 25, which was operating from the airfields at Lérida and Balaguer on the Aragon front. The *Grupo* had been reduced to one squadron, the *Escuadrilla Independiente* Nº 40, and González was appointed *patrulla* CO. This unit operated from the airfields at Tembleque, Camporreal and Madridejos, flying sorties over the Córdoba, Guadalajara, Huesca and Saragossa fronts.

In July, during the battle of Brunete, teniente González was appointed CO of the I-15-equipped 2ª *Escuadrilla* of the *Grupo* Nº 26, successively moving to the airfields at Azuqueca de Henares, Caspe, Alcañiz and

Capitán Chindasvinto González García successively led the 2ª and 1ª *Escuadrillas* of the *Grupo* Nº 26

El Toro. He distinguished himself in air combat during the Belchite offensive when he claimed two CR.32s shot down on 26 August. The following month González was promoted to capitán and confirmed as *escuadrilla* commander. In October he handed over command to deputy CO teniente Gerardo Gil at Alcañiz airfield.

On 7 November capitán Gonzalez resumed command of the 2ª *Escuadrilla* at Figueras airfield, moving with it to Celrá that same day. On the 23rd the unit left the airfield when two patrols were sent to Bujaraloz and the remaining two headed for Candasnos airfield, where all the I-15s were concentrated the following day. On 10 December the 2ª *Escuadrilla* claimed to have downed five CR.32s, one of them falling to González. The remaining four were credited to teniente Calvo and sargentos Castillo, Torn and Martín. Sixteen days later the 2ª *Escuadrilla* transferred to El Toro airfield, and it was while flying from here on 5 January 1938 that González claimed a Bf 109 destroyed as his final recorded aerial victory. His fighter (*Chato* 'CA-002') was hit by anti-aircraft fire while strafing la Muela de Teruel on 8 January, damage to its fuel tanks forcing González to crash land at Sarrión. Three days later he handed over command to teniente Leopoldo Morquillas at Villar airfield.

On 31 January González was ordered to accompany trainee pilots to Kirovabad, returning to Spain on 10 May. In early July he was appointed CO of the 1ª *Escuadrilla* of the *Grupo* Nº 26 in succession to Alesander Stepanovich Osipenko, this unit being based at Manises and Requena airfields during the Levante campaign. According to one of Gonzalez' subordinates, unit deputy CO teniente Juan Sayós, he enjoyed a mixed reputation during his short period in command;

'He was a big, aggressive man. He was authoritarian and did not like his orders being questioned. He gave us instructions about our conduct over the front as if we had never been there before or as though we used to turn tail and run. We were flying a strafing mission over the Sarrión area when we noticed three or four enemy aeroplanes far in the distance. We warned the capitán about the presence of these aircraft and, although there were nine of us, he ordered us to return to base immediately. After we landed we asked him why we had not attacked those fighters. He angrily asked if we had realised that there were 15 or 20 of them. It was obvious that fear had made him see what hadn't actually been there, and that his shouts and his aggressive behaviour was just a mask to hide his cowardice.

'We were ordered to fly top cover for another *escuadrilla*, the *3ª de Chatos*, which had to strafe enemy positions. We were over the target together and, while we flew top cover at 9000 ft, the *3ª Escuadrilla* pilots dived to fulfil their mission, confident that we were covering their backs and would intercept enemy fighters. For a while it looked as though everything was going fine, but some minutes later we saw a group of Fiat fighters heading straight for us, and the capitán ordered us to retreat once again. One after another, all of us formally accused González of desertion in the face of the enemy.'

In light of these events, capitán Chindasvinto González resigned command of the unit on 20 July 1938 and was posted to Alcantarilla airfield. There, he performed the role of test pilot for factory-fresh I-15 *Chatos*, as well as serving as an instructor at the *Escuela de Caza*. González

Alférez Gerardo Gil Sánchez is seen here wearing an unusual mix of rank badges on his uniform. Although the tunic cuff has a braid with a hoop, he has the alférez six-pointed star on his cap, despite this rank having by then been abolished

After leaving the Northern front, teniente Gerardo Gil became *Grupo* N° 26's 2ª *Escuadrilla* CO before eventually serving as an instructor at the *Escuela de Caza* (Fighter School)

was still at Alcantarilla airfield at the end of the civil war, being captured by the victorious Nationalist forces. No further information has come to light on his post-war years.

Gerardo Gil Sánchez

Born in Madrid in 1911, Gerardo Gil Sánchez joined the service in July 1928 and graduated from the *Escuela de Mecánicos* at Cuatro Vientos in December 1930. He was subsequently posted as a cabo mecánico to the *Escuadrilla de Hidros* of the *Fuerzas Aéreas de África* based at El Atalayón. By the outbreak of the civil war Gil had been posted as a cabo mecánico de vuelo (flight engineer) to the *Destacamento de Hidros* of *Grupo* N° 6 at Pollensa, on Majorca. With the island a Nationalist stronghold, Gil was forced to escape in a motorboat on 19 July, being picked up by a Wal flying boat of the Barcelona-based *Aeronáutica Naval*.

From Barcelona he was posted to Los Alcázares and, on 25 August, he joined the *Escuela de Pilotos* at La Ribera. Gil logged 38 hours and graduated as a military pilot in October 1936. After qualifying to fly fighters, he was posted to the Ni-H.52-equipped *patrulla de protección* at Manises. Gil flew several sorties over the Teruel front and in October was promoted to alférez mecánico. In January 1937 he qualified on I-15s and, on 10 February, joined the Spanish *1ª Escuadrilla*, led by capitán Andrés García La Calle. Based at Azuqueca de Henares airfield, the unit operated in the Jarama, Madrid and Guadalajara areas until May. Gil, having been promoted to teniente in March, was then appointed CO of the 3ª *Patrulla* of the *Escuadrilla La Calle*.

In early May the unit moved to Reus following the revolutionary uprising against the Republicans in Barcelona, and once this had been suppressed, Gil took part in the attempt to fly to the Northern front. However, piloting *Chato* '31', he was forced to land at Pau. It was not until 22 May that teniente Gerardo Gil was finally able to lead two I-15 *Chato* elements to La Albericia airfield. Operating from here under the command of teniente Riverola, the aircraft participated in several combats on the Biscay front. In August Gil reported to El Carmolí, where he transitioned to the I-16 *Mosca*, but he did not join the first Spanish I-16 unit because of the arrival of Soviet-trained Spanish pilots from the USSR. He was consequently attached to the *Escuela de Pilotos* at San Javier as an aerobatic flying instructor.

In September teniente Gil was posted to Alcañiz airfield as a deputy commander of the 2ª *Escuadrilla* of the *Grupo* N° 26, being appointed interim CO shortly thereafter. He remained in this temporary post until mid November, flying over the Aragon front from airfields at Venta de Santa Lucía, Sabadell, Reus, Sariñena and Caspe. The most noteworthy action during his period in command of the 2ª *Escuadrilla* was the successful strafing of Garrapinillos airfield, in Saragossa, on 15 October 1937. According to his file, Gil flew nearly 200 sorties during his time in operational units.

After a 25-day leave teniente Gerardo Gil turned over command of the 2ª *Escuadrilla* to teniente Nicomedes Calvo, and by early December he was once again undertaking aerobatic instruction at La Ribera airfield. He remained here until September 1938, when Gil was posted to the *Escuela de Alta Velocidad* at El Carmolí, initially serving under mayor

José González Montero and later mayor Isidoro Jiménez. He flew the school *Moscas* in defensive patrols over Cartagena and operated over Nationalist shipping on 6 March 1939. During the latter mission he was shot at by hostile anti-aircraft artillery on what proved to be his last flight of the war. Taken prisoner by the Nationalists, he was court-martialled and sentenced to 20 years and one day's imprisonment – this sentence was later commuted to ten years. In 1947 Gil was pardoned and settled in Madrid. In the 1980s he was vice-chairman of the *Asociación de Aviadores Republicanos.*

Ladislao Duarte Espés

Born in Erla, Saragossa, on 6 September 1914, Ladislao Duarte Espés enrolled in the flying course at the *Escuela de Vuelo* on 5 January 1937. He logged 16 hours dual elementary instruction and 23 hours solo flying in DH 60s, Farman F.480s and E-34s, followed by 20 hours in Breguet 19s during his advanced training. Duarte subsequently enlisted in the air force as a pilot sargento in April 1937 and undertook the fighter pilots' course. His instructor, teniente Emilio Galera Macías, rated him as 'highly skilled, highly devoted and highly spirited'.

Upon completion of the course Duarte converted onto the I-15 at Madrid and was then posted to the Northern front, where he joined the 3ª *Patrulla* of the *Escuadrilla de Caza del Norte*, commanded by teniente Comas. Flying *Chato* '23', Duarte was promoted to teniente in August 1937. When Miguel Galindo was shot down by an Italian-flown CR.32 on the Santander front on 22 August Duarte became *escuadrilla* CO. The unit subsequently operated from the airfields at Santander, Llanes and Carreño during the offensives on Santander and Asturias, fighting superior numbers of Nationalist aircraft from austere bases. On 30 September teniente Duarte distinguished himself in combat over Gijón with five Bf 109s, the operations record book entry for the day noting;

'At 1330 hrs three biplanes and three monoplanes were scrambled when seven enemy twin-engined aircraft and ten fighters were reported over Gijón. A combat ensued, and one of our monoplane fighters was shot down. It was flown by sargento Daniel Ranz, who was killed. His aircraft was a write-off. The bombers attacked the airfields at Carreño and Vega without result. The *escuadrilla* CO, teniente piloto Ladislao Duarte, and sargento Castillo engaged five monoplanes and deserve praise for their remarkable feat. Their aircraft landed safely although sargento Castillo's was severely damaged.'

Duarte was personally congratulated by the Minister of Defence, Indalecio Prieto, who sent a telegram to the commander of the 6ª *Región Aérea* congratulating him on downing a He 111 and a Bf 109.

Duarte's final combat in the north took place on 18 October while he was on patrol over Gijón. The government fighters engaged Bf 109s and He 111s in a battle that lasted 1 hr 20 min. The I-15 of sargento Miguel Castillo was shot down into the sea near the port, but the aircraft had enough buoyancy to enable the pilot to escape from his cockpit and sit on the tail until he was rescued. The pilots led by Duarte claimed to have shot down two Bf 109s and a He 111. Duarte left the front two days later and, travelling via Biarritz and Toulouse, was held in France for several days.

Having scored several victories on the Northern front, teniente Ladislao Duarte Espés was ordered to establish the 4ª *Escuadrilla* of *Grupo* N° 26 at Gerona airfield, in Figueras

When he finally arrived in Sabadell, Duarte was ordered to establish the 4ª *Escuadrilla* of the *Grupo de Chatos* Nº 26 with the surviving pilots and groundcrews from the Northern front. The unit then patrolled the Barcelona area until being sent to Sagunto airfield to swap its aircraft for those of the 1ª *Escuadrilla de Chatos* that had been flown by Soviet pilots. The latter then returned to the USSR.

Duarte, who had downed another Bf 109 on 20 February 1938, was promoted to capitán on

Ladislao Duarte Espés (in the centre) and two fellow I-15 pilots

7 March and took part in the retreat from Aragon. Flying from Candasnos, his *escuadrilla* claimed two He 111s shot down over the airfield on 10 March, one of which was credited to Duarte for his last aerial success of the civil war. He subsequently led the 4ª *Escuadrilla* during operations in Extremadura, flying from Saceruela airfield in Ciudad Real. On 23 August the commander of the *Escuadra* Nº 11, mayor Isidoro Jiménez, recommended Duarte for the *Medalla del Deber* (Medal for Duty), commending him for his 'extremely high morale and fighting skills' and for being 'highly admired by his comrades for his determination in combat and great leadership qualities'.

On 6 September the 4ª *Escuadrilla* moved to La Señera airfield, in Valencia, but the following day Duarte's aircraft was shot down by anti-aircraft fire while he was making a strafing attack on the Teruel front. The I-15 was set on fire but Duarte managed to bail out behind friendly lines. Although suffering burns, he was rescued by Republican

Teniente Duarte, at the extreme left in the front row, poses with the 4ª *Escuadrilla* groundcrew

infantrymen and spent the next three months in Valencia's El Vedat hospital. Duarte, who was promoted to mayor shortly after being wounded, was succeeded as CO of the 4ª *Escuadrilla* by teniente Emilio Ramírez Bravo. By his own account, Duarte's unit had shot down about 30 enemy aircraft during his time as CO.

Upon being discharged from hospital, Duarte was sent to Catalonia to take command of the *Grupo* Nº 26 in the north as Vicente Castillo Monzó had become CO of both *escuadrillas* in the south. On 5 February 1939 Duarte was at Figueras, but upon defeat by the Nationalists he crossed the Pyrenees into France, where he was interned until he was able to travel to the Soviet Union. He fought with the Red Army Air Force during World War 2, serving in 964 IAP (Fighter Aviation Regiment) with Antonio Arias Arias. Duarte considered returning to Spain in July 1957 but decided against it for fear that he would be jailed. Still living in the USSR in November 1979, he subsequently died there (date and location unknown).

Antonio Nieto Sandoval-Díaz

Until the outbreak of the civil war Antonio Nieto Sandoval-Díaz had been hoping to become an architect. Born in Ciudad Real in 1914, he volunteered instead to become a student pilot, and on 17 January 1937 he sailed for the USSR on board the SS *Ciudad de Cádiz*. Once in Kirovabad he flew Polikarpov U-2s, R-5s and I-5s, before returning to Spain and enlisting in the air force in April. Given the rank of sargento, Nieto was posted to the I-15-equipped 2ª *Escuadrilla* at Archena, but he rarely flew with the unit due to a lack of aircraft.

Together with sargentos Elías Hernández Camisón and Emilio Ramírez Bravo, Nieto subsequently reported to Los Alcázares, where capitán José Riverola was forming a coastal *patrulla* to operate from La Ribera, Alicante, Valencia, Reus and, finally, Figueras. It was at the latter site that teniente Juan Comas established the 3ª *Escuadrilla* of the *Grupo* Nº 26 to fly defensive patrols over the Catalan coast. The unit's initial cadre of pilots consisted of Leopoldo Morquillas, Miguel Zambudio, Juan Olmos, José Redondo, Antonio Britz, Rafael Sanromá Daroca and Antonio Nieto. Later, they were joined by José María Campoamor Peláez, Elías Hernández Camisón, Francisco Montagut Ferrer, Jesús Pérez Pérez, Alfredo de Albert Porcar and José Puig.

The 3ª *Escuadrilla* took part in operations around Teruel, flying from El Toro airfield. Nieto, who was then assigned *Chato* 'CA-017', was promoted to teniente in February 1938 during the battle of Teruel. Leading a *patrulla*, he was active during the retreat from Aragon, flying from airfields at Caspe, Alcañiz, Bujaraloz and Candasnos. Teniente Nieto was appointed CO of the 3ª *Escuadrilla* during Ebro operations in October 1938, succeeding Miguel Zambudio, with teniente Francisco Montagut serving as his deputy. The *escuadrilla* included José Santander, Esteban Corbalán, Sánchez López, José Falcó, Joaquín Tremosa, Álvaro Muñoz, José Garre Solano, Alfredo de Albert, Mario Cuesta, Antonio Britz and Rafael Belda.

In early January 1939 teniente Nieto handed over command of the 3ª *Escuadrilla* to teniente Álvaro Muñoz López and then went on leave, accompanied by capitán Redondo. The pair stayed at a rest home operated

Teniente Antonio Nieto Sandoval-Díaz (left) poses with sargento José Garre Solano of the 3ª *Escuadrilla* at Monjos airfield in Barcelona in late 1938/early 1939

Pilots of the 3ª *Escuadrilla de Chatos* of the *Grupo de Caza* Nº 26 in 1938. They are, from left to right, Antonio Nieto Sandoval-Díaz (*escuadrilla* CO), José Santander Menéndez, unidentified, Antonio Sánchez, Francisco Montagut Ferrer, José Falcó San Martín, Joaquín Tremosa Arnavat, Álvaro Muñoz López, José Garre Solano, Alfredo De Albert Porcal, Mario Cuesta Díaz, Esteban Corbalán Marín and Antonio Britz Martínez

by the *Jefatura de Sanidad* (Health Service) of the *Fuerzas Aéreas* in the city of Camprodon. Subsequently ordered back to Figueras airfield, Nieto was offered one of the new I-15bis *Superchatos* to fly to France, which he did on 6 February 1939 with capitán Emilio Galera Macías as his wingman. The aircraft landed at Carcasonne airfield, near Toulouse, and the two Spanish pilots were interned.

Upon the outbreak of World War 2 seven months later, the Spanish Republicans in France were mobilised into *bataillons de travailleurs*. However, along with other Republican airmen, Antonio Nieto was handed over to the Spanish authorities by the German occupation forces at the border town of Hendaya on 15 July 1940. Sentenced to imprisonment, he was forced to join a penal battalion until his eventual release. The political situation in Spain post-war encouraged Nieto to return to France, where he found employment as a draughtsman in the Marcel Dassault Project Office. Antonio Nieto settled in Anglet, and after retirement he moved to Irún, in Spain.

Álvaro Muñoz López

Born on 10 October 1915 in Irún, Guipuzkoa, Álvaro Muñoz López had been studying for a job in the civil service prior to the arrival of Nationalist troops in his hometown in July 1936. He immediately left for Barcelona by way of France. On 22 December 1936 he volunteered for service as a pilot at La Ribera airfield, undertaking elementary flying training alongside 45 other candidates at Boissy-le-Châtel, in France, between February and July 1937. Here, Muñoz flew Potez 60, MS.341 and C.600 Aiglon aircraft, logging 47 flying hours. After his return to Spain on 25 July 1937, he continued his advanced training on Breguet 19s at La Ribera and finally joined the air force as a pilot sargento in September 1937. Muñoz then trained as a fighter pilot at La Ribera, graduating two months later.

Following a period at the newly established *Grupo de Transición y Eventualidades* (pilot's pool) at Celrá, he was posted on 8 March 1938 to the I-15-equipped 1ª *Escuadrilla* of the *Grupo* Nº 26, the squadron being led by Soviet pilot Aleksander Osipenko. While flying with this unit Muñoz engaged in several successful aerial battles on the Aragon front. He was subsequently posted to the 3ª *Escuadrilla* of the *Grupo* Nº 26 at Monjos airfield, this unit helping to oppose the Nationalist offensive on the Aragon front. Enemy forces were eventually stopped near their

Teniente Álvaro Muñoz López, third from the left, served in the 3ª *Escuadrilla* under Comas, Zambudio and Nieto, before he himself became CO

Teniente Francisco Viñals Guarro, CO of the 2ª *Escuadrilla* of the *Grupo* N° 26, did not seem to care much about the Spanish air force superstition which stated that standing by a propeller was a bad omen – and for good reason, as he was shot down three times but survived unscathed on each occasion

bridgehead over the River Segre. The 3ª *Escuadrilla* was later transferred to the Castellón front, and after seeing action on the Levente front it moved again on 10 August. The unit's pilots also saw action in operations over the Ebro front – it was here on the 21st that Muñoz claimed a CR.32 destroyed.

In September Muñoz was promoted to teniente and, returning from a month's leave on 24 December, he was confirmed as the 3ª *Escuadrilla* CO. He flew sorties over the Catalan front until 8 January 1939, when he and the 3ª *Escuadrilla* moved to the Central-Southern area to participate in the offensive in Extremadura. However, when this operation was cancelled the unit was transferred to Fuenteovejuna, where Muñoz fought several engagements against Nationalist CR.32s. The 3ª *Escuadrilla* was subsequently transferred to La Señera airfield to provide fighter cover for the port of Valencia.

When the victorious Nationalist forces arrived at La Rabasa airfield on 29 March Muñoz surrendered his unit to them. During the civil war Álvaro Muñoz López had logged about 450 flying hours, 340 of them in I-15s. His 200 operational sorties include strafing, frontline patrol, bomber escort and combat missions. Subsequently court-martialled, Muñoz was sentenced to death, although this was commuted to life imprisonment. Eventually released on parole, Muñoz moved to France and lived in Biarritz during the 1970s. The date, and location, of his passing remain unrecorded.

Francisco Viñals Guarro

As a government employee Francisco Viñals Guarro, born in Barcelona in 1915, found himself exempt from military service, but in September 1936 he volunteered for flying training and the following January reported to Alcantarilla airfield. There, he flew DH 60 Moth Majors, before moving on to Breguet 19s. Upon graduation in April 1937 Viñals joined the air force as a pilot sargento, being posted to El Prat de Llobregat to fly Ni-H.52s with the *Patrulla de Protección de Costas* (Coastal Patrol Flight). On 14 August Viñals joined the *Escuela de Alta Velocidad* at El Carmolí for familiarisation training on the I-16 *Mosca*, although he was soon posted as an instructor to the *Escuela Elemental de Pilotos* at Alcantarilla, flying F.480, DH 60 Moth Majors and E-34s.

In early December 1937 sargento Viñals was ordered to Barracas airfield, which was home of the I-15-equipped 1ª *Escuadrilla* of the *Grupo* N° 26, led by Soviet pilot Nikita Timofeevich Susukalov. On the 13th, however, he was transferred to 2ª *Escuadrilla*, commanded by teniente Ladislao Duarte. In January the unit moved from Barracas to El Toro airfield, where teniente Leopoldo Morquillas took charge.

On 21 February, during the battle of Alfambra, Viñals collided with the CR.32 flown by Capitán Carlos Haya, who crashed in government-held territory and was killed. Although Viñals' *Chato* 'CA-013' was badly damaged, he managed to limp back to his airfield and land safely. The aircraft was found to have a shattered aileron, badly damaged upper port wing and missing cockpit door and gunsight. Viñals' promotion, recommended by the *coronel Jefe de Fuerzas Aéreas* and the Minister of National Defence, Indalecio Prieto, was effective from 22 February. The order was gazetted in the *Diario*

Oficial issue No 47, which noted, 'For his heroic conduct in yesterday's combats near Teruel, sargento del arma de aviación D Francisco Viñals Guarro is promoted to teniente'.

Viñals remained with the 2ª *Escuadrilla* of the *Grupo* Nº 26 through to war's end. As a *patrulla* commander, he flew numerous strafing, bomber escort, reconnaissance, frontline patrol and air combat sorties on the Aragon, Levante and Extremadura fronts. While on a sortie from Pomar de Cinca airfield on 24 March 1938, Viñals was shot down by Nationalist CR.32s. He bailed out and landed between Pina and Osera. A short while later the 2ª *Escuadrilla* began a series of moves that would see it flying from a succession of temporary bases – Balaguer, Bell-Puig, Valls, Vendrell (Tarragona), Monjos and Sabanell (Villafranca del Penedés). For the operations in Levante the 2ª *Escuadrilla* flew from Manises, La Señera and, subsequently, Alcublas.

In August 1938 Viñals was sent with his unit to Los Llanos, then to Saceruela and, finally, to La Garganta. Viñals was again shot down in combat during this period, being attacked over the Cabeza del Buey area. On this occasion he managed to land his I-15 on the Almorchón flats. The following day groundcrew repaired the *Chato* and he flew it back to his airfield, despite enemy anti-aircraft fire.

In December Viñals was appointed CO of the 2ª *Escuadrilla* shortly before the start of operations in Catalonia. The unit also saw action over Extremadura and Pozoblanco in 1939, one of its pilots being credited with downing the Nationalist CR.32 of high-scoring ace Capitán Manuel Vázquez Sagastizábal on 23 January.

On 29 March teniente Viñals led a formation of 12 I-15s of the 2ª *Escuadrilla* to Barajas airfield, where the unit formally surrendered its equipment to the victorious Nationalist armies. Viñals was later court-martialled and sentenced to 25 years' imprisonment. The sentence was commuted to eight years, but he was pardoned after serving two years and three months. Viñals settled in Barcelona, where he died in 2011.

Pilots of the *2ª Escuadrilla de Chatos* of the *Grupo de Caza* Nº 26 at Sabanell airfield in Villafranca del Penedés, Barcelona, in 1938. Standing in flying helmets, from left to right, are Francisco Viñals Guarro (*escuadrilla* CO), Gregorio Montoro (chief of staff, squatting), Antonio Menéndez Martínez, Rafael Belda Linares and José Brufau Basanta. Lying, from left to right, are Antonio Sánchez, Jaime Torn Roca and Francisco Sagasti Fernández

Teniente Francisco Viñals boards his *Chato* at Sabanell airfield

I-16 MOSCA GRUPO Nº 21

The first batch of 31 I-16s arrived in Spain from the Soviet Union in November 1936, and the monoplane fighters would soon make their presence felt at a time when the Republican hold on Madrid was hanging by a thread thanks to the speed of the Nationalist drive on the Spanish capital.

At first the fast new fighters, nicknamed *Moscas*, were flown only by Soviet pilots. Indeed, it was not until the summer of 1937 that the first Spanish pilots, graduates of the Soviet flying school at Kirovabad, returned home to fly the modern fighter in combat. Pilots who had trained at local schools also began their conversion onto the *Mosca* at the special I-16 *Escuela de Alta Velocidad* located at El Carmolí airfield. Initially they were instructed by Soviet pilots, but the latter were soon joined by Spanish personnel. Indeed, the school's first CO was capitán Isidoro Jiménez, who had accompanied the Spanish pilots to the USSR.

The autumn of 1937 saw the formation of an all-Spanish I-16 unit, the 1ª *Escuadrilla,* commanded by El Carmolí graduate capitán Manuel Aguirre. It was soon followed by the 4ª *Escuadrilla*, led by recently promoted teniente Manuel Zarauza. When Aguirre was appointed to command the *Grupo* Nº 21 he was succeeded by the Soviet-trained teniente Eduardo Claudín. The four Soviet-manned *escuadrillas* were 2ª, 3ª, 5ª and 6ª, and tactical deployment of the whole *grupo* was controlled by the Soviets. The *Grupo* Nº 21, however, gradually became a wholly Spanish unit. On 10 April 1938 the 3ª *Escuadrilla*, which had been disbanded by the Soviet command, was reactivated under the command of teniente José María Bravo Fernández, who was another first year graduate from the USSR. Shortly thereafter the Soviet-led 6ª *Escuadrilla* was also disbanded, only to be reactivated under teniente Francisco Meroño Pellicer's command during the battle of the Ebro.

Two other Soviet-manned *escuadrillas,* 2ª and 5ª, merged in September 1938 to become the 5ª *Escuadrilla*, which was manned by second year Soviet-trained Spanish pilots. A new Spanish *escuadrilla* (7ª) was formed under teniente José Puig Torres during the battle of the Ebro

A newly delivered, unidentified, *Mosca*. The I-16 was the fastest fighter in the government air force

67

to operate overhauled Type 6 I-16s. The other *escuadrillas* of the *Grupo* Nº 21 were re-equipped with 90 Type 10 *Moscas* from the last batch of I-16s to arrive in Spain via France.

In October 1938 the Soviet pilots of the *Grupo* Nº 21 left Spain, but by then command of the 5ª *Escuadrilla* had already been entrusted to a Spaniard, teniente Julio Pereiro Pérez. The leadership structure of the *Grupo* is detailed below;

Spanish COs of the *Grupo* Nº 21 *Mosca escuadrillas*

Grupo Nº 21
Manuel Aguirre López
Eduardo Claudín Moncada
Manuel Zarauza Clavero

1ª *Escuadrilla*
Manuel Aguirre López
Eduardo Claudín Moncada
José Redondo Martín
Enrique Vilatela Soria
José María Cano Arnaiz

2ª *Escuadrilla*
Soviet manned (disbanded in September 1938)

3ª *Escuadrilla*
José María Bravo Fernández
Francisco Tarazona Torán
Antonio Calvo Velasco

4ª *Escuadrilla*
Manuel Zarauza Clavero
Antonio Arias Arias

5ª *Escuadrilla*
Soviet manned (merged with 2ª *Escuadrilla* in September 1938)
Julio Pereiro Pérez

6ª *Escuadrilla*
Francisco Meroño Pellicer

7ª *Escuadrilla*
José Puig Torres

The first of the Spanish I-16 pilots to distinguish themselves in combat were Aguirre, Claudín, Zarauza and Bravo.

Manuel Aguirre López
Born in Madrid on 22 March 1907, Manuel Aguirre López enrolled at the *Escuela de Mecánicos* at Cuatro Vientos in September 1926. As a soldado mecánico, he took a flying course and was awarded his wings in

November 1929. Aguirre's first posting as a cabo piloto was to the *Servicios del Material* (Equipment Command) and later, as a sargento, he joined the *Escuadra* Nº 3 of the *Grupo de Reconocimiento* Nº 23 at Logroño, equipped with Breguet 19s. He later graduated as a fighter pilot and flew Ni-H.52s with the *Grupo* Nº 13 at Barcelona.

In July 1936 sargento piloto Aguirre was posted to the 2ª *Escuadrilla* of the *Grupo de Caza* Nº 12. Commanded by capitán José Méndez, the unit was transferred to Getafe, and after the outbreak of war Aguirre took part in aerial combat over the Sierra and Talavera fronts. Credited with shooting down a CR.32 on 2 September, Aguirre was rewarded for his success with promotion to alférez a little over three weeks later. That month, too, he was transferred with his Ni-H.52 '3-74' to Andújar and the 1ª *Escuadrilla* of the re-established *Grupo* Nº 21. This was a mixed unit, equipped with Breguet 19 bombers and Nieuport fighters, and during battles over the Córdoba front Aguirre claimed another CR.32.

Promotion to teniente followed in November, and he began flying more modern I-15 *Chatos* of the 1ª *Escuadrilla*, which at that time was led by Ivan Kopets. Aguirre flew as a member of the *patrulla* led by Soviet pilot Kosakov, and when the latter established his own *escuadrilla*, Aguirre was appointed *patrulla* CO. The new squadron initially flew from El Soto airfield, after which it moved to Málaga and then on to Almería. Aguirre subsequently fought in the battle of Guadalajara.

On 1 April 1937 he was posted to the short-lived *Grupo de Caza Chatos* Nº 16, flying over the Aragon front as a member of Kosakov's *escuadrilla*. On 11 June, after a month's sick leave, Aguirre led a *patrulla* of four I-15s, flown by teniente Fernández de Velasco and sargentos Zarauza and Montagut. Whilst attempting to deliver reinforcements to government fighter units operating in the Biscay area, all four pilots were forced to land at the French airfield at Parme, in Biarritz. The aircraft were seized but their pilots were allowed to return to Spain.

Aguirre became one of the first Spanish pilots to fly an I-16 when he joined the first conversion course at El Carmolí in August 1937 with, among others, sargento Manuel Zarauza. Later that same month, during the battle of Belchite, he was appointed *patrulla* CO in the 1ª *Escuadrilla*, which was led successively by Soviet pilots Snr Lt Boris Smirnov and Nikolai Ivanov. Aguirre was promoted to capitán and given command of the 1ª *Escuadrilla* of the *Grupo* Nº 21 in September.

On 12 October Aguirre claimed to have shot down a CR.32 and, just before the battle of Teruel, on 8 November, he was appointed to lead both Spanish *escuadrillas* of *Grupo de Moscas* Nº 21 – 1ª and 4ª, commanded by tenientes Eduardo Claudín and Manuel Zarauza, respectively. The *grupo* had a further four *escuadrillas* – 2ª, 3ª, 5ª and 6ª, – all of them led by Soviet ace Capt Ivan Eremenko.

Capitán Manuel Aguirre López was the first Spanish commanding officer of an *escuadrilla* (the 1ª *Escuadrilla*) within the I-16 *Mosca*-equipped *Grupo* Nº 21

Aguirre (on the right) was appointed deputy commander of the *Escuadra de Caza* under mayor Isidoro Jiménez (left). They are flanking capitán José María Bravo, deputy commander of the *Grupo* Nº 21

In April 1938, after Catalonia was cut off from the rest of Republican-held territory, the 3ª *Escuadrilla* became wholly Spanish under the command of teniente José María Bravo Fernández. Aguirre, whose I-16 was coded 'CM-137', was now leading three *escuadrillas*. He finally relinquished command of *Grupo* Nº 21 on 18 June, by which time he had been credited with ten aerial victories – two CR.32s while flying Ni-H.52s, one Ju 52/3m, three He 51s and one CR.32 flying *Chatos* and one He 111, one Bf 109 and one CR.32 flying *Moscas*. Aguirre was succeeded as CO of *Grupo* Nº 21 by Eduardo Claudín, who was killed in action soon afterwards. The latter was then replaced by Manuel Zarauza.

On 21 July Aguirre was posted to the *Jefatura de la Sección de Parque y Experimentación* (Test Branch Command and Depot) at Manlleu airfield, and then on 11 September he was appointed deputy commander of the *Escuadra de Caza* Nº 11. He was replaced by fellow ace capitán Andrés García La Calle on 24 October. By then Aguirre had been promoted to mayor. In January 1939 he returned to Catalonia, but after its fall to the Nationalists he escaped across the Pyrenees into France.

Following the German occupation of Vichy-controlled southern France, Aguirre was returned to Spain on 3 April 1944. Court-martialled, he was sentenced to 20 years' imprisonment, although he was released on parole in 1945. Aguirre then settled in Madrid, where he died some years later.

Eduardo Claudín Moncada

As a student aeronautical engineer, Eduardo Claudín Moncada was admitted to the *Escuela Superior Aerotécnica* (School of Aeronautics) in October 1935 as part of the government-sponsored four-year plan. He was the son of comandante de Artillería Fernando Claudín Jareño, who had been forced into retirement by the Azaña Bill. Claudín's brother, also called Fernando, was an alférez de navío (sub-lieutenant) in the navy, and he had been murdered for his support of the military uprising whilst serving aboard the battleship *Jaime I*. Yet both Eduardo and his father remained loyal to the government, and both reported for duty on the outbreak of war. Comandante Fernando Claudín later commanded the *Regimiento de Artillería* of the 1ª *División* of the so-called *Exèrcit de Catalunya* (Catalan Army) and, with promotion to coronel, was appointed artillery chief.

Despite his youth, the tall Eduardo Claudín was highly educated and fluent in English, French and German. He was also the holder of a glider pilot's licence. When Spain descended into civil war Claudín was in Barcelona, and he soon joined the *Escuela de Aviación del POUM* – a flying school established by the POUM Marxist militias to prepare student pilots for admission to the *Aviación Militar*. When an official flying training course was gazetted, he left the school to apply.

It is unlikely that the Soviet contingent in Spain was aware of Claudín's flirtation with a party affiliated to the International Revolutionary Marxist Centre, as this could have put him in serious trouble with the Stalinists. Indeed, Claudín undertook the first year of his flying training course in the USSR, sailing from Cartagena on board the SS *Ciudad de Cádiz* on 17 January 1937. Fifteen days later he landed in Feodosia, in the Crimean peninsula, for the journey to Kirovabad, via Rostov and Tbilisi. In June Claudín returned to Spain, which entailed a sea journey from Leningrad to Le Havre and a railway trip through France. He attended the *Escuela de Alta Velocidad* at El Carmolí for conversion training to the I-16 and, after a brief spell in an I-15 unit, was posted to the 1ª *Escuadrilla de Moscas*, led successively by Soviet pilots Ivan Devotchenko, Boris Smirnov and Nikolai Ivanov and Spanish ace Manuel Aguirre López.

Claudín soon became popular with his comrades, and he also attracted the favourable attention of his superiors. This led to his promotion to teniente in November 1937, making him the first pilot of his year to achieve such rank.

During the battle of Teruel (which commenced in December 1937) Claudín commanded the 1ª *Escuadrilla*. The unit included a few survivors of the fighting on the Northern front like sargento Luis de Frutos, who would be killed during the unit's operations from Sarrión airfield. The squadron later moved to Liria, in Valencia, and on 20 January 1938 Claudín claimed a CR.32 destroyed while flying from here. His normal mount at this time was *Mosca* 'CM-157'. For his leadership of the 1ª *Escuadrilla* during the Teruel campaign Claudín was promoted to capitán in March 1938.

That same month the Nationalists launched their offensive in Aragon, south of the Ebro. The 1ª *Escuadrilla* quickly returned to its old airfield at Caspe, where it was greeted by He 111s of the *Legion Condor* – two *Chatos* were destroyed in the ensuing raid. During those days of hard fighting Claudín's unit operated alternately from airfields at Almenar (Lérida), Bell-Puig and Reus. On 10 March his pilots claimed a He 111, which force-landed and was set on fire by its crew prior to their capture. On 15 March Claudín shared in the destruction of a CR.32, but sargento Tarazona had to make a belly landing following the action.

On 9 April the unit left the Aragon front for Barcelona to provide support for the new Minister of National Defence, Dr Juan Negrín. Claudín and his men flew from airfields at Valls, Salou and Sagunto until May, when the 1ª *Escuadrilla* commenced operations on the Castellón front from Liria. Fresh pilots replaced unit veterans at this time, the latter being transferred to teniente José María Bravo's re-formed 3ª *Escuadrilla*.

Having claimed a share in the destruction of a Bf 109 on 14 June, Claudín was appointed CO of the *Grupo* Nº 21 the following day in succession to capitán Manuel Aguirre. It was to be a short-lived appointment, however. Flying over the Teruel front on 5 July, Claudín perished when his *Mosca* was hit by Nationalist anti-aircraft fire and crashed in enemy-held territory near Villaestar. His posthumous promotion to mayor was dated 7 July 1938.

Capitán Eduardo Claudín Moncada successively commanded the 1ª *Escuadrilla* and the *Grupo* Nº 21 de Moscas

Claudín, a tall *Ingeniería Aeronáutica* student, spoke several languages. Posing with him in this photograph is Jose María Bravo, CO of the 3ª *Escuadrilla de Moscas*

Manuel Zarauza Clavero

Born at Santoña, in Santander, on 3 November 1917, Manuel Zarauza Clavero was one of the most successful fighter pilots of the civil war – indeed, he may well have been the ranking Republican ace. At the time of the military uprising he was serving as a private in Cuatro Vientos. In November 1936, having been promoted to sargento, Zarauza attended the *Escuela de Pilotos Militares* at La Ribera. His graduation, in January 1937 according to his personal documentation, was never gazetted. Zarauza's records also state that during his training he flew a variety of aircraft types – DH 60 Moth Major, E-34, Breguet 19, Miles M 2 Hawk, C.600 Aiglon, Fleet 10, GL.32, Avro 626, Morane-Saulnier MS.341, Koolhoven FK.51 and Ni-H.52 – logging 88 hr 12 min flying time.

After completing the fighter pilots' course on 12 February 1937, Zarauza was rated by comandante Félix Sampil, CO of the *Escuela de Caza*, as an 'exceptionally gifted pilot' – high praise from one who had already seen operational service. After his training Zarauza was posted to the Spanish-manned and I-15-equipped 2ª *Escuadrilla*. Commanded by capitán Roberto Alonso Santamaría, the unit participated in operations at Guadalajara, Cerro de Garabitas (Madrid) and Teruel. In May 1937 Zarauza took part in both attempts to send fighter reinforcements to the Northern front via France. His first effort, on the 8th, ended in a landing at Toulouse in *Chato* '54', but on the 17th engine trouble forced him to turn back. He tried again on 11 June, and this time the four pilots led by teniente Manuel Aguirre landed at Parme airfield, in Biarritz. The aircraft were interned and the pilots sent back to Spain.

Zarauza was then sent on a *Mosca* conversion course at the *Escuela de Alta Velocidad* at El Carmolí, which ended on 31 August 1937. He was posted to the *Grupo* Nº 21 at Caspe and joined Ivanov's 1ª *Escuadrilla* on 25 September. Thanks to his exceptional piloting skills, Zarauza was promoted to teniente in November and later made CO of the 4ª *Escuadrilla de Moscas*. The

Pilots of the 4ª *Escuadrilla de Moscas* of the *Grupo de Caza* Nº 21 in 1938. They are, from left to right, Pedro Rueda Barcia, unidentified, Manuel Zarauza Clavero (*escuadrilla* CO), unidentified, unidentified, unidentified, Manuel Fernández Ferreiro, Armando Ortega Velilla, unidentified and José Díez Tejedor

Pilots of the 4ª *Escuadrilla de Moscas* of *Grupo de Caza* Nº 21 in 1938. Standing, from left to right, are José Díez Tejedor, unidentified, unidentified, unidentified, unidentified and Pedro Rueda Barcia. Squatting, from left to right, are unidentified, unidentified and Manuel Zarauza Clavero

unit was deployed to Alcalá de Henares for the defence of Madrid, and in late November its pilots found themselves up against Bf 109s. After a move to Santa Cruz de la Zarza airfield for operations on the Central front, they took part in the battle of Teruel, flying from the airfields at Villar and Sarrión. On 22 January teniente Zarauza shot down a Bf 109, followed by a second one on 29 March. The latter month also saw him promoted to capitán.

Zarauza continued to lead the 4ª *Escuadrilla* – also known as the 'Popeye' squadron through its adoption of the cartoon character whose image was displayed on the fins of its aircraft – and participated in the campaigns in Aragon and Levante. According to an official biographical sketch published in the Barcelona newspaper *El Diluvio* on 12 June 1938, Zarauza had by then participated in about 100 aerial battles and shot down 23 enemy aircraft, a total which included fighters and bombers.

During the Valencia offensive Zarauza succeeded capitán Eduardo Claudín as CO of the *Grupo* Nº 21. His appointment was dated 23 July 1938, and he remained in this position until the fall of Catalonia four months later. As CO of the 4ª *Escuadrilla*, Zarauza usually flew I-16 'CM-125' and later *Mosca* 'CM-225', which was assigned to the *grupo* staff. He flew extensively during the battle of the Ebro (fought between July and November 1938), taking it in turns with deputy CO capitán José María Bravo to lead the *escuadrillas*. Promoted to mayor in September, Zarauza remained continuously on duty without taking leave throughout the key battles of 1938. And during the 500 flying hours of operational flying he clocked up that year he avoided being shot down or even wounded.

Short in stature, Zarauza was one of the youngest Republican squadron COs – he was barely 22 when he was promoted to comandante. Fellow high-scoring ace Francisco Tarazona Torán wrote that Zarauza would hunch down in his cockpit, thus earning himself the nickname of piloto fantasma or 'ghost pilot'. He was irascible, but also liked to play tricks with his pistol. It has been said that when teniente coronel Valentín González (commander of the 46ª *División*) moved his headquarters to a country estate that the *grupo* had been ordered to vacate Zarauza threatened to take off and strafe it. He was dissuaded from doing so by his comrades. Zarauza also tossed a smoke canister into the mess during a dinner in the presence of *Aviación Militar* 'top brass' and Soviet

Capitán Manuel Zarauza Clavero commanded the *Grupo de Caza* Nº 21 from July 1938 until the end of hostilities

The famous I-16 Type 10 'CM-225' that was usually flown by mayor Zarauza during the autumn of 1938

commanders. Yet many, including his subordinates, considered him to be both a good leader and a valiant pilot.

Catalonia's fall into Nationalist hands prompted Zarauza to escape to France together with most of his pilots. He was interned at Argelès-sur-Mer and Gurs, but later settled in the USSR and joined the Red Army Air Force on the outbreak of the Great Patriotic War. Capt Zarauza commanded an *eskadrilya* of 961st IAP until he was killed on 12 October 1942 in a mid-air collision with his wingman, Sgt Alcxander Riapishev, over the airfield of Kishli, in Baku. A monument to him was erected in the cemetery where he was interred.

José María Bravo Fernández

José María Bravo Fernández was born in Madrid on 8 April 1917 into a liberal minded family who later enrolled him in the freethinking *Institución Libre de Enseñanza.* There, he became fluent in French and German, and was also a successful sportsman. Bravo subsequently joined Madrid's *Aéreo Popular* flying club and learned to fly gliders. As he was preparing for admission to the *Escuela de Ingenieros de Caminos* (Civil Engineering College) war broke out. Holidaying in Santander at the time, he volunteered for service in the air force at La Albericia airfield. Bravo was able to fly some operational sorties in teniente Hernández Franch's DH 89 Dragon Rapide and José María Carreras' Fokker F.VII/3m tri-motor in August, but he was discharged in September by capitán Manuel Cascón, commander of the *Fuerzas Aéreas del Norte*, for not being an official recruit.

Bravo eventually reached Catalonia via France, whereupon he considered applying to become an observer until his friend José María Carreras suggested that that he should learn to fly instead. After joining the flying course at Los Alcázares, Bravo left for the USSR on 17 January 1937 together with Claudín, Arias, Meroño and Tarazona. Returning to Spain in May, he was initially posted in error to a *Chato escuadrilla*, but after a few sorties he was sent to Belchite to join the 1ª *Escuadrilla de Moscas* of the *Grupo* Nº 21. Bravo soon became a *patrulla* commander, but also flew with *grupo* CO Valentin Ukhov. Claiming his first two victories (both CR.32s) on 25 and 26 September, Bravo downed another Fiat fighter on the Aragon front on 12 October followed by a floatplane ten days later.

In December 1937, in recognition of his outstanding flying skills and leadership qualities, Bravo was appointed deputy *escuadrilla* CO under Claudín. He claimed a Bf 109 over the Teruel front on 22 January 1938, followed by a half-share in the destruction of a second Messerschmitt fighter on 7 February. In March Bravo was promoted to teniente.

On 10 April the 3ª *Escuadrilla de Moscas* was officially reformed with

A widely publicised photo of Bravo, who was then the 3ª *Escuadrilla* CO, being shaved by his engineer Álvaro Padín next to I-16 *Mosca* 'CM-193'

Capitán José María Bravo Fernández, posing with the groundcrew assigned to service his aircraft

José María Bravo Fernández in flying gear at Vendrell airfield between missions

Spanish personnel, and Bravo was made CO. He appointed two course mates from the USSR, Francisco Tarazona and Restituto Toquero (both Northern front veterans), and José Alarcón from Murcia as *patrulla* commanders. The other members of the *escuadrilla* were Vicente Yuste and Andrés Fierro, both from Madrid, Francisco Paredes and Vicente Beltrán from Valencia and Pedro Utrilla and Luis Sirvent from Aragon.

Having claimed four more victories in late April, José María Bravo was rewarded with promotion to capitán on 28 May. His 3ª *Escuadrilla*, also known as *Seis Doble* (Double Six) after the domino artwork displayed on the fins of its aircraft, operated from Sagunto airfield for the whole of the Castellón campaign. It also flew from El Vendrell during a Nationalist attack on the Balaguer bridgehead and from Camporrobles towards the end of the battle for Valencia. Finally, there was a period of duty at La Rabasa, from where patrols were flown over the port of Valencia. During the early weeks of the battle of the Ebro the unit operated from el Plá de Cabra airfield. Bravo was again amongst the victories during this spell of intense action, claiming two Bf 109s and two CR.32s destroyed between 20 June and 24 August.

On 27 August Bravo handed over command of the 3ª *Escuadrilla* to sargento Francisco Tarazona and was appointed deputy CO of the *Grupo* Nº 21 under Zarauza. He remained in this position until the end of the campaign in Catalonia, flying up to four sorties a day as he led his *grupo* throughout the battle of the Ebro. Bravo claimed his final victory on 3 November when he downed a Bf 109.

Capitán José María Bravo Fernández, CO of the *Grupo* Nº 21 in 1938-39

The following month he accompanied teniente coronel Juan Quintana Ladrón de Guevara to the international airshow in Paris to view the Polish PZL P.37 Los bomber that had been ordered by the Republican government. It was to be a brief respite from the hard fighting.

Upon his return to Spain Bravo took part in the campaign in Catalonia, and on 6 February 1939, when most of the Republican fighters had been lost in combat or destroyed on the ground, he left for France. Accompanied by his pilots and groundcrewmen, Bravo walked across the Pyrenees and was interned at Argelès-sur-Mer.

Bravo's logbook shows that he flew 1100 hours in Republican fighters during the civil war. Logging 1120 operational sorties, mostly in I-16s coded 'CM-129', 'CM-193' and 'CM-249', he took part in 160 aerial combats and claimed to have shot down 23 enemy aircraft individually and shared (probables are also included in this tally). Despite seeing so much action, Bravo never had to bail out of his aircraft and suffered no serious incidents in combat.

Following his freedom from internment, Bravo left for the Soviet Union to resume his engineering studies. In the wake of the German invasion of the USSR in June 1941, he joined the Red Army, serving with a mining engineers' unit that carried out dangerous missions behind enemy lines. A chance meeting with a Soviet general who had also fought in Spain resulted in Bravo being asked to list the 50 or so Spanish airmen that he knew who were scattered among different units of the Red Army. These men were subsequently ordered to join the air defence force.

Capt José María Bravo Fernández duly served with the 3rd Fighter Squadron of 481st IAP, VIII Army Corps. Eventually commanding the unit, he also led 485th and 961st IAPs, but there are no records to indicate whether he claimed any aerial victories. Bravo and Antonio Arias Arias were among the pilots who escorted Stalin's Lisunov Li-2 to Tehran and back in November and December 1943. He flew later I-16 variants, as well as Spitfires, Hurricanes, Kittyhawks and Airacobras. Upon his demobilisation in 1948, Bravo held the rank of lieutenant colonel, his wartime service having added 630 flying hours to his logbook.

Following his discharge from the Red Army Air Force, Bravo worked at a Moscow language school and became its vice-dean. In 1960 he was finally able to return to Spain to be reunited with his family. Bravo duly published his memoirs, and received the Order of Zhukov from the Russian ambassador to Spain. This decoration, presented to senior officers for outstanding military leadership during the Great Patriotic War, was awarded to just 100 combat veterans between 1995 and 1998. Bravo remained active up until his death in Madrid on 26 December 2009, aged 94.

Antonio Arias Arias

Born in Madrid on 29 April 1915, Antonio Arias Arias was a printer who, despite working for the monarchist newspaper *ABC*, was also a militant member of the *Juventud Socialista Unificada* and took part in the October 1934 print workers' strike in Madrid. He was arrested and jailed, but released in the February 1936 amnesty and able to return to work. On the outbreak of the civil war Arias volunteered for the *Batallón Fernando de Rosa* militia and fought on the Sierra de Peguerinos front. He then decided to become a pilot, and on 17 January 1937 Arias left for the Soviet Union to participate in the flying course at Kirovabad.

Graduating as an I-16 pilot, Arias joined Ivan Devotchenko's Soviet *escuadrilla* in August. Here, he served alongside Eduardo Claudín Moncada, Ramón Gandía, Joaquín Velasco, José María Bravo, Antonio Pérez, José Alarcón, Fernández Alberdi, José Ruiz and Jiménez Marañón. Arias was assigned *Mosca* 'CM-093', which he flew over Aragon during the summer and autumn of 1937, when capitán Manuel Aguirre assumed command of the unit. By then Arias, who usually flew I-16 'CM-158', had two and one shared kills and two unconfirmed claims to his name.

November saw the formation of the Spanish 4ª *Escuadrilla de Mosca*, commanded by teniente Manuel Zarauza and with sargento Arias as

Capitán Antonio Arias Arias commanded the 4ª *Escuadrilla de Moscas* until the end of hostilities

deputy CO. A number of new pilots joined the unit at this time, including Marciano Díaz, Julio Pereiro, Sabino Cortizo, José Puig and Ortega Velilla. Initially, they operated in the Central area, flying from the airfields at Alcalá de Henares and Santa Cruz de la Zarza. In mid-December the 4ª *Escuadrilla* moved to Villar airfield, in Valencia, and fought in the battle of Teruel. Claiming 1.5 Bf 109s and a CR.32 destroyed in January-February 1938, Arias

Arias, squatting in the middle of the front row, is seen with his pilots and groundcrew of the 4ª *Escuadrilla*

remained in the thick of the action until 24 February. During the final stages of the battle he crashed while taking off in *Mosca* 'CM-025'. Seriously injured, Arias was admitted to hospital in El Vedat.

In April, during his convalescence at the *Casa de Reposo de Aviación* at La Malvarrosa, Arias was promoted to teniente. After 56 days in hospital he rejoined his unit, whereupon he discovered that government-held

territory had been cut in two by the Nationalists. Arias took part in the Levante campaign and the offensive on Valencia, flying from Camporrobles airfield. In late July, by which point he had been credited with a further three and two shared victories since late April, Arias succeeded Zarauza in command of the 4ª *Escuadrilla de Mosca*. On 30 July the unit was transferred to El Vendrell airfield for operations over the hotly contested Ebro front.

The *Moscas* of the 4ª *Escuadrilla*, all of which featured a 'Popeye' artwork on their fins, were fitted with supercharged Wright-Cyclone R-1820-F4 engines to improve their performance at higher altitudes. Higher ceilings meant that pilots now had to wear oxygen masks, and the latter led to the 4ª *Escuadrilla* being given a new nickname – *la del chupete* (dummy)

Capitán Arias Arias climbs out of his I-16 *Mosca* 'CM-260'. He flew this machine throughout the battle of the Ebro, using it to claim his final three victories (all Bf 109s) in Spain

Ninety new Type 10 *Moscas* arrived in Spain during the early summer of 1938 to make good losses suffered by Republican units, but Arias' *escuadrilla* only received five examples as the aircraft in his unit had already been fitted with more powerful Wright-Cyclone R-1820-F4 engines to improve the I-16's performance at higher altitudes. Higher ceilings meant that pilots now had to wear oxygen masks, and the latter led to the 4ª *Escuadrilla* being given a new nickname – *la del chupete* (dummy).

Throughout the battle of the Ebro Arias was assigned Type 10 *Mosca* 'CM-260', and he used it to claim his final three victories in Spain. These successes led to him being promoted to capitán in October 1938.

The bitter fighting in Catalonia, which started in late December, virtually wiped out the *escuadrilla*. In February 1939 Arias and his surviving pilots crossed the border to France on foot. Like many other Republican fighter pilots, he was able to leave for the USSR after a brief period of internment. Upon the outbreak of the Great Patriotic War, Arias joined the Red Army Air Force and was posted to a special unit flying captured German aircraft. He subsequently flew MiG-3 fighters in the defence of Moscow, and by 1942 Arias was commanding the 2nd Fighter Squadron of 964th IAP/130th AD. Having flown Hurricanes and Tomahawks on the Leningrad front, Arias served with 740th IAP and later became an observer with 439th IAP.

Demobilised in 1948, Arias settled in Minsk and returned to his job as a printer. He travelled back to Spain in 1990 and died there after publishing his memoirs.

José Redondo Martín

The son of Socialist leader and mayor of Madrid Cayetano Redondo Aceña, José Redondo Martín applied for pilot training and, in December 1936, was one of 50 Spaniards posted to a civilian flying school in France as part of an agreement between the two nations. Redondo enrolled at the Hanriot School at Bourges, where he flew Potez Po.25s and Hanriot H.172s, H.182s and H.437s in order to gain a French pilot's licence. Upon his return to Spain in April 1937 he took a further course at La Ribera on Breguet 19s and graduated as a sargento the following month.

In July Redondo was posted to the I-15-equipped 2ª *Escuadrilla* following the battle of Brunete, the unit having been transferred to Sariñena for the fighting in the Belchite area. He was mentioned in dispatches on 26 August as follows;

'A major air battle over the Aragon front near Saragossa this morning ended in complete success for the Republican air force, which managed to shoot down five enemy aeroplanes – four Fiats and a Romeo – without loss to our *escuadrillas*. Worthy of mention in this combat is the conduct of a recently graduated sargento, José Redondo, son of the former mayor of Madrid, Cayetano Redondo. In combat with a Fiat, Redondo shot it down, despite numerous machine gun hits to his own aircraft, several of which damaged its port wing. After shooting down the Fiat Redondo flew his aircraft the considerable distance back to his airfield. The groundcrew found it hard to understand how Redondo had managed to make it to their airfield with such damage to his fighter aircraft and a serious leg wound.

'The Minister of National Defence congratulated the heroic pilot, and in the presence of all the personnel of the fighter *escuadrillas* at the airfield, promoted him to teniente. Several captured enemy airmen stated that our offensive in Aragon had occupied a great deal of the aviation forces operating on the Santander fronts. One of the captured airmen, comandante Pérez Pardo, has a serious stomach wound and is in hospital.'

Redondo's promotion was confirmed on 13 September, and he was posted to the 3ª *Escuadrilla* of the *Grupo* Nº 26 under teniente Juan Comas, who was just a few days his senior. As a member of this unit, Redondo took part in the operations in Teruel and Aragon, before attending the *Escuela de Alta Velocidad* at El Carmolí to participate in an I-16 conversion course. Following Claudín's death on 5 July 1938 Redondo was given command of the 1ª *Escuadrilla* of the *Grupo* Nº 21 at Camporrobles airfield in mid July. It was at around this time that he was involved in a collision with a Bf 109 during an engagement over the Levante front, the Spaniard being forced to take to his parachute. Redondo reached friendly lines two days later.

On 9 August the 1ª *Escuadrilla* collected 12 brand new Type 10 *Moscas* (coded 'CM-211' to 'CM-226') from Celrá and took them to Vendrell airfield, where the unit was based for Ebro operations. Redondo's *escuadrilla* did not start the battle well. At 1740 hrs on 14 August the unit's pilots engaged a force of 12 He 111s and 30 CR.32s, and although the Republicans claimed several victories they lost two *Moscas* and sargentos Rubén Gómez Redondo and Sirio Martín González to landing accidents at Vendrell.

On 21 August the 1ª *Escuadrilla* received reinforcements in the form of four new *Moscas* from the 3ª *Escuadrilla*. The following day the unit was ordered to fly to the Central-South area, where its pilots operated from Liria airfield before moving to Almodóvar del Campo. On 2 September they were escorting the 4ª *Escuadrilla de Katiuskas* when a formation of Nationalist CR.32s was engaged. Redondo, in 'CM-214', was shot down by Capitán Ángel Salas Larrazábal. Bailing out, he was escorted to the ground by Salas in his circling CR.32. Redondo gestured at his conqueror with a clenched fist, which the Nationalist pilot answered with the Fascist salute. Redondo landed behind friendly lines and was able to rejoin his *escuadrilla*.

The I-16s returned to Liria, then known as *Aeródromo* 424, where they remained until 9 September when 15 aircraft departed for Reus airfield for operations over the Ebro front.

On 1 November the 1ª *Escuadrilla* of the *Grupo* Nº 21 scored a confirmed victory over a Nationalist CR.32 when teniente Redondo and teniente José María Cano Arnáiz of the 5ª *Escuadrilla* (flying Mosca 'CM-198') were given shared credit for downing the Fiat fighter near Fatarella Hill, the machine crashing in flames. The following day Redondo's

Capitán José Redondo Martín fought on the Extremadura and Ebro fronts. After undergoing a course at the *Escuela de Alta Velocidad,* he was appointed CO of the 1ª *Escuadrilla de Moscas* in mid July 1938

A rare photograph of an I-16 *Mosca* in flight, the aircraft appearing to be on short finals for landing

1ª *Escuadrilla* also shot down a Bf 109, which crashed on the sierra at Tirisa. There was a further engagement on the 9th when the 1ª and 6ª *Escuadrillas de Moscas* attacked enemy twin-engined aircraft, forcing them to break formation and dive for their own lines. One of the bombers crashed in flames after being attacked by teniente Enrique Vilatela south of Fatarella, while sargento Santamaría downed a CR.32. But these successes were not without cost, as the *escuadrilla* lost *Mosca* 'CM-238' of teniente Juan Sayós, while 'CM-244' sustained a damaged propeller.

It was at about this time that teniente José Redondo handed over command of the *escuadrilla* to teniente Enrique Vilatela. The former, who had claimed a share in the destruction of a Bf 109 on 28 December as his final success, was to remain without a command until war's end. Redondo escaped to France, where he was interned at Argelès-sur-Mer until he fled to Costa Rica. Subsequently working as a pilot for a local company, he eventually settled in Mexico and found employment as a factory manager. In 1989 Redondo's Spanish citizenship was restored and he was granted the status of a retired coronel in the *Ejército del Aire*. He returned to Spain and died in Benidorm, Alicante, in 1998.

Francisco Tarazona Torán

Although Francisco Tarazona Torán was born in Mexico City on 21 June 1915, his parents were Spanish and they returned home to settle in Valencia when he was still a child. Working as a draughtsman when the civil war commenced, Tarazona soon volunteered to serve the Republican cause as a pilot. On 17 January 1937 he sailed for the USSR on board the SS *Ciudad de Cádiz* and subsequently joined the flying course at Kirovabad. Returning to Spain in June, Tarazona attended the *Escuela de Alta Velocidad* at El Carmolí and was promoted to sargento piloto in April. He then became a member of the 2ª *Patrulla* of the recently established *escuadrilla de Moscas*, led by Soviet pilot Boris Smirnov.

In August 1937 Tarazona flew with his unit from Alcalá de Henares to La Albericia to reinforce the fighter force on the Northern front. There, he was quick to demonstrate his skill as a fighter pilot, downing a CR.32 on the 17th of that month and a Bf 109 on the 27th. However, on 13 October Tarazona was himself shot down near Gijón. Taking to his parachute, he landed in a tree in enemy-held territory and made his way to Valencia, via France, to recover from his wounds.

In March 1938 Tarazona was posted to the 1ª *Escuadrilla* of *Grupo de Moscas* Nº 21, based at Liria airfield and subsequently at Caspe for the defence of the Aragon front during the Nationalist offensive. Having claimed a share in the destruction of a CR.32 with this unit on 15 March, Tarazona was posted to the recently re-formed 3ª *Escuadrilla* – the *Seis doble* of *Grupo* Nº 21 *de Moscas* – and appointed *patrulla* CO on 10 April. He duly participated in the campaign in Levante while based at Sagunto and Camporrobles, claiming four and

Francisco Tarazona (closest to the camera) attended the first *Mosca* course for Republican pilots in the USSR

three shared victories and one unconfirmed success from 25 April through to 24 August.

During the latter month capitán José María Bravo was promoted to deputy *grupo* CO, and Tarazona – then still a sargento – assumed command of the 3ª *Escuadrilla*, which he led in the aerial engagements during the battle of the Ebro. He was promoted to teniente in September (having been credited with one and one shared CR.32 victories that month) and confirmed as *escuadrilla* CO. In October Tarazona claimed one and three shared victories, followed by another success in November, but on 8 December he was injured when his *Mosca* ('CM-249') suffered engine failure while taking off from Valls. After a short spell in hospital, Tarazona returned to Catalonia to fly *Mosca* 'CM-193'. He claimed his last success in this machine on 30 December when he downed a Bf 109. On 7 February 1939 Tarazona was lucky to escape with his life when 'CM-193' was attacked by *Legion Condor* aircraft while he was attempting to take off from Vilajuiga.

As Republican resistance crumbled the high-scoring ace sought refuge in France. Thanks to his Mexican nationality, Tarazona was able to return to Mexico and join his family there. Francisco Tarazona Torán later found employment as a captain with the airline *Mexicana*, flying Douglas DC-3s, DC-4s and DC-6s, de Havilland Comet 4s and Boeing 727s. After retirement from the flightdeck, he served as an air service inspector at the airline's headquarters at Mexico City international airport, before becoming operations manager for the *Servicios Aéreos de la Comisión Federal de Electricidad*. Tarazona then established the Francisco Tarazona Flying School, which he ran until he retired to Cuernavaca. He died there on 1 July 1988.

Francisco Tarazona logged a total of 23,300 flying hours and was awarded the Emilio Carranza medals for reaching 10,000 and 15,000 commercial flying hours. He was also a successful author, displaying a meticulous, precise style in numerous articles published in magazines and newspapers like *Hélice*, the magazine of the *Asociación Sindical de Pilotos Aviadores* (ASPA – Pilots' Trade Union). Tarazona also wrote two books,

Capitán José María Bravo Fernández (left) poses with his successor as CO of 3ª *Escuadrilla de Moscas*, teniente Francisco Tarazona Torán. Both men were highly experienced aviators who subsequently served with the Red Army Air Force in World War 2

The *Moscas* of the 3ª *Escuadrilla*, then led by Tarazona, prepare to take off at the start of yet another combat sortie over the Ebro front

the first, entitled *Sangre en el cielo* (*Blood in the Sky*) and published by Costa Amic in Mexico City in 1958, was an account of his experiences in the civil war. It was also published in Spain by Editorial San Martín in 1974 – while the country was still ruled by General Franco – under the title *Yo fui piloto de caza rojo* (*I was a Red Fighter Pilot*). His second book, *El despertar de las águilas* (*Eagles Awake*), detailed the history of the ASPA, of which Tarazona was an enthusiastic member and office holder.

In his book *Blood in the Sky*, Tarazona stated that he had scored six individual aerial victories and some shared with other pilots during the civil war. The author interviewed Francisco Tarazona during a visit to Spain in 1988 and, after checking documentary sources and consulting renowned historians such as American Thomas Sarbaugh, he believes that Francisco Tarazona Torán scored at least eight aerial victories and another eight shared with Eduardo Claudín Moncada, Antonio Calvo Velasco, José María Bravo Fernández and Manuel Montilla y Montilla.

Francisco Meroño Pellicer

Born in Mula, Murcia, on 17 June 1917, Francisco Meroño Pellicer was working as a surveyor on the River Mundo power station construction site when the war broke out. He volunteered for service in the government militias in Albacete and suffered a leg wound in the subsequent fighting. After convalescence he moved to Madrid, and in December 1936 he went to Los Alcázares as a student pilot. On 17 January 1937 Meroño sailed from Cartagena for the USSR on board the SS *Ciudad de Cádiz*, subsequently graduating as a fighter pilot at Kirovabad and returning to Spain in June with the rank of sargento. After further training at El Carmolí he was posted to a Soviet I-16 *escuadrilla* in July for operations over the Madrid front.

In August sargento Meroño was transferred to the 1ª *Escuadrilla* of the *Grupo de Moscas* Nº 21, commanded by capitán Manuel Aguirre and based at Caspe airfield. From here he served on the Aragon front, flying mainly reconnaissance and frontline patrol sorties. While flying *Mosca* 'CM-061' on 10 March 1938 Meroño downed a He 111 that was attacking Caspe airfield. Later that month he was promoted to teniente. In August the 6ª *Escuadrilla de Moscas* was reformed and Meroño was appointed CO.

The new unit of the *Grupo* Nº 21 included veterans like teniente Juan Huertas Garcíafrom and Primitivo Pérez Gómez, as well as the newly qualified sargentos José Carbonell Balaguer, Manuel Fernández Ferreiro, Antonio García Cano, Francisco Ortega Casado, Juan Cebrián Motada, Fernando Morales Escamilla, Francisco Castelló Poveda, Antonio Cano Cano, Rafael Izquierdo Pascual, José Ramón Fernández González and Manuel Morató Arias. All had been on the second year flying course in the USSR. They were joined by sargentos Francisco Arroyo Adarbe and José Serrato Serrato.

The 6ª *Escuadrilla* played an active role in the battle of the Ebro and recorded notable success during the bitter fighting. Indeed, Meroño claimed four and one shared victories between 14 August and 31 October, and this success saw him promoted to capitán. Little is known about his subsequent career from late 1938 except that he flew to the USSR after the war ended and died in Moscow on 17 July 1995.

Capitán Francisco Meroño Pellicer distinguished himself whilst leading the 6ª *Escuadrilla* of the *Grupo* Nº 21 during the Levante and Ebro campaigns

REPUBLICAN NIGHTFIGHTER FORCE

The first dedicated nightfighter sorties of the Spanish Civil War were flown by Soviet pilots during the final phase of the battle of Brunete in late July 1937, Maj Mikhail Yakushin and future ace Snr Lt Anatoliy Serov both claiming to have shot down *Legion Condor* Ju 52/3ms conducting night bombing raids over the Madrid front.

When war broke out there were no fighter units on either side specifically formed for night operations. From late 1936 Republican bomber units were equipped with R-5 *Rasantes* for nocturnal bombing missions, with the *Escuela de Vuelo Nocturno* (Night Flying School) being established at El Carmolí to train Spanish crews in the operation of these machines. Koolhoven FK.51s, Hanriot H.431s and Breguet 19s were the unit's primary equipment.

The first night success for a Spanish Republican pilot came in the early hours of 21 March 1938 when sargento José Sarrió took off from Reus in a D.510 (one of only two in Spain) and during the ensuing sortie shot down a He 59B seaplane, killing the crew.

Apart from their use as trainers, the Koolhoven FK.51s of the *Escuela de Vuelo Nocturno* at El Carmolí were also used for night coastal defence patrols. Two aircraft were written off flying these missions, the first of which was FK.51 'EK-008'. Sargento Francisco Sánchez Matos scrambled in this aircraft from El Carmolí at 0030 hrs on 7 June 1938, but he was forced to crash-land when his engine seized due to oil starvation. The FK.51 turned over in front of the base hospital and Sánchez was wounded and the aircraft destroyed. At 0005 hrs on 19 June FK.51 'EK-013', flown by sargento Juan Cobo Becerril, took off from El Carmolí and dived into the Mar Menor a short while later for no apparent reason, killing the pilot.

In late 1938 the *Patrulla de Caza Nocturna* was established, equipped with the versatile I-15 *Chato*. The unit's Polikarpov biplane fighters were progressively modified over coming weeks through the fitment of landing lights and special exhaust pipe collector rings. The squadron

A well known photograph of an I-15 of the *Escuadrilla de Caza Nocturna* – the unit charged with the nocturnal defence of the Catalan coastline – being refuelled

– whose first CO was teniente Walter Katz, followed by teniente José Falcó San Martín – was given the task of defending the Catalan coastline from bases at Canudas (El Prat de Llobregat) and Sabadell airfields.

Walter Katz

Although born in Germany, Walter Katz held Spanish nationality. As a volunteer with a private pilot's licence, he was readily accepted as a military pilot in September 1936 and posted to the 1ª *Escuadrilla* of the *Grupo* Nº 21, equipped with Breguet 19s. The unit was deployed to Andújar to fly reconnaissance and bombing missions over the Córdoba front. Sorties were also flown over the Nuestra Señora de la Cabeza sanctuary, in Jaén, where the province's rebel *Guardia Civil* forces were besieged under the command of capitán Santiago Cortés.

In October 1936 Katz became a brigada, after which he was posted to Manises and he continued flying Breguet 19s, as well as a Latécoère 28, on coastal reconnaissance sorties. In March 1937 he was promoted to teniente after the alférez and brigada ranks were abolished. Katz was subsequently posted to the R-Z *Natacha Grupo* Nº 25 and, after its disbandment in June 1937, to the *Escuadrilla Independiente* Nº 50. The latter unit was commanded by Isidoro Jiménez, with Katz being appointed CO of one of its flights.

After the battle of Brunete, an *Escuadrilla de Bombardeo Nocturno* (night bombing squadron) was established to harass the Nationalists by operating single-aircraft sorties behind enemy lines at 15 to 20-minute intervals. Equipped with 12 R-5 *Rasantes*, the unit was led by teniente Walter Katz from Bujaraloz airfield, in Aragon.

In early May 1938 teniente Katz was ordered by the *Subsecretaría de Aviación* to undertake a secret mission to Paris, where he was almost certainly tasked with purchasing night flying equipment. He flew to London on the 4th, leaving for Paris via Boulogne. Remaining in the French capital until 4 June, Katz returned to Barcelona via Cerbère after a 16-day trip.

In late 1938 Katz was appointed CO of the *patrulla de caza nocturna* equipped with I-15 fighters fitted with landing lights. The *patrulla* normally operated in the Catalan area from El Prat de Llobregat, with occasional detachments to Valencia. On 11 November teniente Katz was shot down and killed by anti-aircraft fire during a night attack on the Serós bridgehead on the left bank of the River Segre. He had been accompanied on the mission by sargento López Fernández, who escaped the intense flak unscathed. After Katz' death command of the nightfighter *patrulla* passed to teniente José Falcó. Katz was posthumously promoted to capitán with effect from 1 September.

Teniente Walter Katz (second on the left) was the first CO of the *Escuadrilla de Caza Nocturna*. This rare photograph shows him with some of his pilots

Although a successful nightfighter pilot, Teniente José Falcó claimed most of his victories while serving with the 3ª *Escuadrilla de Chatos* – a day fighter unit

Teniente José Falcó San Martín climbs into the cockpit of one of his usual mounts, I-15 'CA-058' of the 3ª *Escuadrilla de Chatos*

Teniente José Falcó succeeded Katz as CO of the *Escuadrilla de Caza Nocturna* after the latter was killed in combat on 11 November 1938. Falcó was promoted to capitán after shooting down two Bf 109s over Vilajuiga on 6 February 1939 – his last sortie in the civil war

José Falcó San Martín

A mechanic by trade, José Falcó San Martín was born in Barcelona on 27 September 1916. Serving in the Spanish navy when war broke out, he passed the necessary entrance examination and was able to join the air force as a student pilot in March 1937. Falcó started the elementary phase of his flying course at Alcantarilla airfield in June, flying DH 60 Moth Majors, before moving first to La Ribera and then to Los Alcázares, where he graduated as a pilot on 31 October 1937. He was posted to the *Cuadro Eventual de Pilotos* (pilot's pool) at Celrá, flying I-15 *Chatos*.

In March 1938 Falcó found himself a member of the short-lived 5ª *Escuadrilla de Chatos*, which was disbanded the following month. He was then posted to the 3ª *Escuadrilla*, led by capitán Juan Comas. It was during his service with this unit that he logged a total of 366 flying hours and fought in 20 aerial combats. In April alone Falcó claimed eight victories, of which five were confirmed – three CR.32s, a Bf 109 and a He 59. On 19 June he was credited with downing a CR.32 on the Levante front, while on 1 August, at Vinaroz, Falcó claimed a second He 59 destroyed.

Falcó also performed night operations while serving with the 3ª *Escuadrilla*, and in September his aerial successes earned him promotion to teniente. By mid-November he had assumed command of the I-15-equipped *Patrulla de Vuelo Nocturno*, based at Canudas airfield (El Prat de Llobregat). He succeeded teniente Walter Katz on 11 November 1938.

Falcó fought to the end in Catalonia, and during his last sortie, on 6 February 1939, he shot down two Bf 109Es over Vilajuiga airfield, in Gerona. These victories, over Hans Nirminger (6-96) and Heinrich Windemuth (6-98), were followed by promotion to capitán. Falcó fled to France four days later,

Teniente Falcó (in the centre of this group) poses with four of his *Escuadrilla de Caza Nocturna* pilots

where he was interned in Boulou, Argelès-sur-Mer and, finally, Gurs, near Oloron-Sainte-Marie. Falcó had a relative living in Algeria, so he was eventually allowed to settle there. Rejected for service in the *Armée de l'Air*, Falcó received French citizenship in 1953 and, following Algeria's colonial war, he moved to Toulouse to work as a mechanic for the gendarmerie until retirement in 1976. The death of Franco and the end of the dictatorship in Spain saw Falcó's rights restored, and he became a coronel de la reserva in 1980. He remains an active member of the ADAR veterans' association today.

José Sarrió Calatayud

José Sarrió Calatayud, who was born at Navarret, in Valencia, on 11 January 1919, had previously worked as a carpenter prior to enlisting in the air force as a sargento pilot in July 1937. After taking the fighter pilots' course at the *Escuela* at La Ribera and spending time in the replacement pool at Celrá, he was posted to the 1ª *Escuadrilla* of *Grupo de Defensa de Costas* Nº 71. There, he was assigned one of the two D.510s of the Reus *patrulla*, which had been established on 21 February 1938.

An unidentified D.510TH of the *Grupo de Defensa de Costas* – the Republicans had just two examples of the Dewoitine monoplane fighter on strength. Sarrió was flying one of these aircraft when he shot down a He 59 seaplane of the *Legion Condor* on 21 March 1938

Teniente Jose Sarrió receives the congratulations of coronel Hidalgo de Cisneros, commander in chief of the Republican *Fuerzas Aéreas*, after his night victory on 21 March 1938

On 5 March Sarrió flew D.510 'CW-001' to La Cenia airfield before returning to Reus, where he was scrambled after enemy aircraft were sighted over Tarragona. He flew another intercept mission – this time at night – three days later, but the 'enemy' aircraft turned out to be a Republican R-5 *Rasante* bomber. On 9 March six Savoia bombers attacked Reus, and both D.510s were scrambled. Neither fighter managed to catch the raiders, however. Sorties were flown almost daily, but no combats were recorded until the night of 21 March, when sargento Sarrió managed to shoot down a He 59 seaplane of the *Legion Condor's* AS./88 near Cambrils, in Tarragona. The *Boletín de Información del Sector Aéreo de Reus* noted;

'At 0425 hrs enemy air activity was reported near Reus, and a Dewoitine was scrambled from this airfield. A combat ensued over Cambrils with two seaplanes, one of which was shot down – it crashed on the road from Cambrils to Hospitalet. Four crewmen were killed, and a German survivor was taken to hospital at Cambrils but he died 40 minutes later. The wreckage indicates that the aircraft is of the same type as the one shot down a few days earlier at Vinaroz, namely a twin-engined Heinkel seaplane. The aircraft was completely destroyed in the ensuing fire. The other seaplane, which was forced to drop its bombs over the sea, returned to Palma. It too had been hit, but our aircraft was not able to continue the pursuit for lack of ammunition. Our aircraft landed safely.'

The following day Sarrió was promoted to teniente by Order No 4.356, which stated;

'In recognition of his conduct in shooting down a Heinkel twin-engined aircraft near Cambrils last night, sargento D José Sarrió Calatayud is promoted to teniente de Aviación.'

Sarrió was personally congratulated by the commander of the *Fuerzas Aéreas*, coronel Hidalgo de Cisneros. He was then posted to the I-15-equipped 1ª *Escuadrilla* of *Grupo* Nº 26, then still under the command of Soviet pilot Osipenko. In spite of Sarrió's promotion, Osipenko assigned him to a *patrulla* that was led by a sargento, which the newly acclaimed hero failed to appreciate. A short while later Sarrió was shot down in combat on the Levante front, although he was able to safely take to his parachute.

On 2 October, however, teniente Sarrió's luck finally ran out and his I-15 'CA-188' was downed over the Ebro. Although he managed to bail out of his stricken biplane over no-man's-land, Sarrió was apparently killed in the crossfire between Republican and Nationalist troops once on the ground.

APPENDICES

SPANISH REPUBLICAN ACES

Manuel Zarauza Clavero (4ª/21)

22/1/38	Bf 109
29/3/38	Bf 109

Notes – According to his semi-official biography supplied to the press by the *Jefatura de Fuerzas Aéreas*, Zarauza scored a total of 23 victories, although the two Bf 109s listed above are the only ones confirmed by type and date. This figure includes his individual score of five, as well as those victories claimed with his *escuadrilla*. Unless hitherto unknown official documents come to light, it is virtually impossible to take the matter further. The documentation pertaining to Zarauza's World War 2 service in the USSR also remains undiscovered. According to unofficial sources, he shot down seven enemy aircraft while flying with 961st IAP. There is no confirmation of this, however, and some historians consider these to be shared victories.

Francisco Meroño Pellicer (1ª and 6ª/21)

10/3/38	He 111
14/8/38	CR.32
21/9/38	CR.32
21/9/38	CR.32
3/10/38	CR.32
31/10/38	Bf 109 (half-share)

Notes – According to his memoirs, capitán Meroño scored a total of 20 victories, although the kills listed above are the only ones confirmed by type and date. The details of his World War 2 service in the USSR remain unknown.

Vicente Castillo Monzó (2ª and 1ª/26)

18/7/37	He 51
24/8/37	CR.32
24/8/37	CR.32
26/8/37	CR.32
26/8/37	Ro.37
2/9/37	CR.32
2/9/37	CR.32
10/12/37	CR.32
7/38	CR.32
9/38	Bf 109
9/38	CR.32
9/38	CR.32
9/38	CR.32

José Falcó Sanmartín (3ª/26 and *Vuelo Nocturno*)

19/6/38	CR.32
10/7/38	He 59 (night)
1/8/38	He 59 (night, unconfirmed)
21/8/38	He 59 (night, unconfirmed)
23/9/38	Bf 109
24/9/38	SM.79 (unconfirmed)
1/11/38	CR.32
2/11/38	CR.32
18/11/38	He 59 (night)
17/12/38	He 59 (night, unconfirmed)
31/12/38	He 59 (night)
17/1/39	He 59 (night, unconfirmed)
6/2/39	Bf 109
6/2/39	Bf 109 (unconfirmed)

Manuel Aguirre López (1ª/21)

2/9/36	CR.32
12/10/37	CR.32
Unknown	CR.32
Unknown	CR.32
Unknown	Ju 52/3m
Unknown	He 51
Unknown	He 51
Unknown	He 51
Unknown	He 111
Unknown	Bf 109

Notes – According to his statement to the author, Aguirre shot down ten enemy aircraft, although only the first two listed above can be confirmed by date.

Antonio Arias Arias (1ª and 4ª/21)

26/8/37	He 111 (half-share)
2/9/37	CR.32
5/9/37	unspecified enemy aircraft
9/37	CR.32 (unconfirmed)
12/10/37	CR.32 (unconfirmed)
4/1/38	Bf 109 (half-share)
1/38	CR.32
5/2/38	Bf 109
29/4/38	Bf 109

13/5/38	CR.32
6/38	Do 17 (half-share)
6/7/38	CR.32
7/38	Bf 109 (half-share)
13/8/38	Bf 109
21/8/38	Bf 109
31/12/38	Bf 109 (half-share)

Notes – During World War 2 Arias was credited with a shared Ju 88 (on 26 September 1941) and a confirmed Ju 88 (on 21 June 1943) destroyed whilst serving in the USSR. He was awarded the Order of the Red Banner and the Order of the Patriotic War 1st and 2nd class.

José María Bravo Fernández (1ª and 3ª/21)

25/9/37	CR.32
26/9/37	CR.32 (half-share)
12/10/37	CR.32 (unconfirmed)
22/10/37	floatplane
22/1/38	Bf 109
7/2/38	Bf 109 (half-share)
21/4/38	He 111
25/4/38	He 111 (half-share)
25/4/38	Bf 109
27/4/38	SM.79
10/6/38	Bf 109 (half-share)
18/7/38	Bf 109
19/7/38	CR.32 (half-share)
24/8/38	CR.32
3/11/38	Bf 109

Notes – The details of Bravo's service in the USSR in World War 2 remain unknown.

Francisco Tarazona Torán (3ª/21)

17/8/37	CR.32
27/8/37	Bf 109
15/3/38	CR.32 (half-share)
25/4/38	He 111
11/5/38	Bf 109
10/6/38	Bf 109 (half-share)
14/6/38	Bf 109 (half-share)
4/7/38	SM.79
19/7/38	CR.32 (half-share)
14/8/38	He 111 (unconfirmed)
24/8/38	CR.32
21/9/38	CR.32
22/9/38	CR.32 (half-share)
16/10/38	2 CR.32s (credited to *patrulla*)
30/10/38	CR.32
31/10/38	He 111 (credited to *patrulla*)
7/11/38	Do 17 (set on fire)
30/12/38	Bf 109

Andrés García La Calle (1ª/11)

25/7/36	Breguet 19
30/8/36	Ju 52/3m
31/8/36	CR.32
2/9/36	Ju 52/3m
11/36(?)	He 51
13/2/37	He 51
18/2/37	He 51

Notes – According to *Alas*, the official Republican aviation magazine, La Calle 'destroyed six rebel aircraft and forced a further five to land, some behind our lines and others on the enemy side'.

Felipe Del Río Crespo (*Escuadrilla de Chatos del Norte*)

28/12/36	DH 89
4/1/37	Ju 52/3m
13/4/37	*Legión Cóndor* twin-engined bomber
18/4/37	Do 17
20/4/37	Breguet 19
Unknown	Unknown
Unknown	Unknown

Notes – According to the *Jefatura de las FF.AA. del Norte* ORB, prior to his death, capitán Felipe Del Rio Crespo had achieved seven confirmed victories.

Juan Comas Borrás (3ª/26)

17/4/37	He 51 (damaged)
28/12/37	CR.32
28/12/37	CR.32
30/12/37	Bf 109
20/1/38	Bf 109
3/38	CR.32
Unknown	Unknown
Unknown	Unknown

Notes – Comas certainly achieved more individual victories, although they are not recorded in operational record books. According to his own statement, he had scored seven confirmed victories and some probables.

Chindasvinto González García (2ª/26)

26/8/37	CR.32
26/8/37	CR.32
10/12/37	CR.32
5/1/38	Bf 109
Unknown	Unknown

Ladislao Duarte Espés (*Escuadrilla de Caza del Norte* y 4ª/26)

30/9/37	Bf 109
30/9/37	He 111
20/2/38	Bf 109
10/3/38	He 111

Notes – According to Duarte's own statement, the 4ª *Escuadrilla* claimed a collective total of 30 aircraft destroyed, which included his own individual score of four victories. Details of his World War 2 combat record in the USSR remain unknown.

Leopoldo Morquillas Rubio (2ª/26)

17/4/37	He 51
17/1/38	CR.32
18/1/38	Bf 109
20/1/38	CR.32 (damaged)
21/2/38	CR.32 (unconfirmed)

Notes – The above victories are reported in the diary of the *Escuadra* Nº 11. Morquillas must have scored more victories during the periods for which there is no precise information. Details of his World War 2 combat record in the USSR remain unknown.

Miguel Zambudio Martínez (3ª/26)

8/37	Bf 109
10/12/37	He 111 (half-share)
22/2/38	Bf 109 (unconfirmed)
4/38	CR.32

Notes – In a letter to the author in 1978, Zambudio stated that he had shot down 23 aircraft while serving with his unit and approximately as many probables. However, the kills listed above are the only ones that can be identified by type and date.

Jaime Torn Roca (2ª/26)

10/12/37	CR.32
20/1/38	Bf 109
1/11/38	CR.32
1/11/38	CR.32 (half-share)

Notes – Torn scored further, unrecorded, victories. However, the kills listed above are the only ones that can be identified by type and date.

Eduardo Claudín Moncada (1ª/21)

Unknown	Unknown
Unknown	Unknown
20/1/38	CR.32
15/3/38	CR.32 (half-share)
14/6/38	Bf 109 (half-share)

Notes – Claudín certainly scored at least two further victories before January 1938, but details for these kills have not come to light.

José Redondo Martín (1ª/21)

26/8/37	CR.32
1/11/38	CR.32 (half-share)
28/12/38	Bf 109 (half-share)

Notes – Redondo should be regarded as an ace as he achieved further, unrecorded, victories.

Spanish Republican Fighter Pilots' Claims as based on surviving official records from mid-October 1937 to late January 1939

Escuadra de Caza Nº 11 War Diary

Date	Pilot	Unit	Aircraft type
12/10/37	M Aguirre López	1ª/21	CR.32
12/10/37	A Arias Arias	1ª/21	CR.32 (probable)
12/10/37	J M Bravo Fernández	1ª/21	CR.32 (probable)
12/10/37	R Gandía	1ª/21	CR.32 (probable)
12/10/37	M Lamas Quevedo	2ª/26	CR.32
12/10/37	García	2ª/26	CR.32
22/10/37	??	1ª/21	Seaplane
25/10/37	J J Armario	PM/26	SM.81 (half-share)
4/11/37	??	2ª/26	Twin-engined seaplane
30/11/37	??	4ª/21	He 111
30/11/37	??	4ª/21	He 111
10/12/37	C González García	2ª/26	CR.32
10/12/37	V Castillo Monzó	2ª/26	CR.32
10/12/37	J Torn Roca	2ª/26	CR.32
10/12/37	A Martín García	2ª/26	CR.32
10/12/37	N Calvo Aguilar	2ª/26	CR.32
10/12/37	M Zambudio Martínez	2ª/26	He 111 (half-share)
10/12/37	A Britz Martínez	2ª/26	He 111 (half-share)
28/12/37	J Comas Borrás	3ª/26	CR.32
28/12/37	J Comas Borrás	3ª/26	CR.32
28/12/37	F Montagut Ferrer	3ª/26	CR.32
28/12/37	R Sanromá Daroca	3ª/26	CR.32
30/12/37	J Comas Borrás	3ª/26	Bf 109

30/12/37	J Baldero Escudero	3ª/26	Bf 109
5/1/38	C González García	2ª/26	Bf 109
5/1/38	E Ramírez Bravo	2ª/26	CR.32 (damaged)
16/1/38	*Patrulla*	4ª/21	SM.81
17/1/38	L Morquillas Rubio	2ª/26	CR.32
17/1/38	J Vela Díaz	2ª/26	CR.32
17/1/38	C Zuazo Garre	2ª/26	CR.32
18/1/38	L Morquillas Rubio	2ª/26	Bf 109
20/1/38	*Escuadrilla*	4ª/21	Bf 109
20/1/38	*Escuadrilla*	4ª/21	Bf 109
20/1/38	*Escuadrilla*	4ª/21	Bf 109
20/1/38	*Escuadrilla*	1ª/21	He 111
20/1/38	J Fernández Alberdi	1ª/21	Bf 109
20/1/38	J Fernández Alberdi	1ª/21	Bf 109
20/1/38	E Vilatela Soria	1ª/21	Bf 109
20/1/38	Fernández	1ª/21	Bf 109
20/1/38	*Escuadrilla*	1ª/21	Bf 109
20/1/38	E Claudín Moncada	1ª/21	CR.32
20/1/38	J Solinas Figueras	1ª/21	CR.32
20/1/38	J Torn Roca	2ª/26	Bf 109
20/1/38	I Morquillas	2ª/26	CR.32 (damaged)
20/1/38	M Brufau Civit	2ª/26	CR.32 (damaged)
22/1/38	J M Bravo Fernández	1ª/21	Bf 109
22/1/38	M Zarauza Clavero	4ª/21	Bf 109
6/2/38	*Escuadrilla*	1ª/21	Bf 109
7/2/38	??	??	3 x Bf 109s
20/2/38	L Duarte Espés	4ª/26	Bf 109
21/2/38	??	1ª/21	CR.32
21/2/38	J Mora Fauría	2ª/26	CR.32
21/2/38	C Zuazo Garre	2ª/26	CR.32
21/2/38	F Viñals Guarro	2ª/26	CR.32
21/2/38	L Morquillas Rubio	2ª/26	CR.32 (probable)
21/2/38	F Villins León	2ª/26	CR.32 (probable)
21/2/38	F Montagut Ferrer	3ª/26	Bf 109
21/2/38	??	4ª/26	CR.32
22/2/38	C Zuazo Garre	2ª/26	Bf 109 (probable)
22/2/38	M Zambudio Martínez	3ª/26	Bf 109 (probable)
8/3/38	*Escuadrilla*	1ª/21	He 111 (probable)
10/3/38	F Meroño Pellicer	1ª/21	He 111
10/3/38	*Escuadrilla*	3ª/26	CR.32
10/3/38	*Escuadrilla*	3ª/26	Bf 109
10/3/38	*Escuadrilla*	4ª/26	He 111
10/3/38	*Escuadrilla*	4ª/21	Bf 109
12/3/38	*Escuadra*	Nº 11	3 x CR.32s (strafed)
14/3/38	*Escuadra*	Nº 11	6 x CR.32s
15/3/38	*Escuadra*	Nº 11	CR.32
15/3/38	*Grupo*	2ª & 3ª/26	3 x CR.32s
16/3/38	*Escuadra*	Nº 11	2 x He 51s
19/3/38	*Escuadra*	Nº 11	CR.32
20/3/38	J Pérez Chulvi	4ª/21	Seaplane
24/3/38	*Escuadra*	Nº 11	4 x CR.32s
24/3/38	*Escuadra*	Nº 11	Bf 109
24/3/38	*Escuadra*	Nº 11	CR.32 probable
24/3/38	*Escuadra*	Nº 11	He 51 probable
29/3/38	M Zarauza Calvero	4ª/21	Bf 109

Escuadra de Caza Nº 11 and *Jefatura de Fuerzas Aéreas* War Diaries

6/4/38	*Escuadrilla*	4ª/26	CR.32
8/4/38	*Escuadrilla*	1ª/21	CR.32
13/5/38	*Escuadra*	Nº 11	8 x CR.32s
13/5/38	*Escuadra*	Nº 11	2 x Bf 109s
14/5/38	*Grupo*	Nº 21	2 x Bf 109s
15/5/38	*Escuadra*	Nº 11	CR.32 (set on fire)
15/5/38	*Escuadra*	Nº 11	Bf 109
19/5/38	*Escuadra*	Nº 11	4 x Bf 109s
19/5/38	*Escuadra*	Nº 11	Do 17
23/5/38	*Escuadra*	Nº 11	CR.32
23/5/38	*Escuadra*	Nº 11	He 111
26/5/38	*Escuadra*	Nº 11	4 x CR.32s
26/5/38	*Escuadra*	Nº 11	12 x CR.32s (probables)
31/5/38	*Escuadra*	Nº 11	10 x CR.32s
4/6/38	*Escuadra*	Nº 11	Bomber
7/6/38	??		2 x Bf 109s
9/6/38	??		9 x CR.32s
9/6/38	??		Bomber
11/6/38	??		2 x Bf 109s
14/6/38	??		3 x Bf 109s
14/6/38	??		He 111
15/6/38	??		4 x Bf 109s
15/6/38	??		Bomber
21/6/38			4 x CR.32s
26/6/38	??		2 x Bf 109s

Escuadra de Caza Nº 11 War Diary

Date	Pilot	Unit	Aircraft type
24/9/38	*Escuadrilla*	5ª/21	CR.32
24/9/38	*Escuadrilla*	6ª/21	CR.32
24/9/38	*Escuadrilla*	6ª/21	CR.32
24/9/38	*Escuadrilla*	6ª/21	CR.32
24/9/38	*Escuadrilla?*	*Grupo* Nº 21	Bf 109
27/9/38	*Escuadrillas*	4ª and 5ª/21	2 x Bf 109s
2/10/38	*Escuadrilla?*	*Grupo* Nº 21	CR.32
2/10/38	*Escuadrilla?*	*Grupo* Nº 21	CR.32
2/10/38	*Escuadrilla?*	*Grupo* Nº 21	3 x CR.32s (probables)
3/10/38	*Escuadrilla*	1ª/26	CR.32
3/10/38	*Escuadrilla*	1ª/26	CR.32
3/10/38	*Escuadrilla*	1ª/26	CR.32
3/10/38	*Escuadrilla*	3ª/26	CR.32
3/10/38	*Escuadrilla*	4ª/21	CR.32
3/10/38	*Escuadrilla*	4ª/21	CR.32
3/10/38	*Escuadrilla*	4ª/21	CR.32
3/10/38	*Escuadrilla*	7ª/21	CR.32
3/10/38	*Escuadrilla*	7ª/21	CR.32
3/10/38	*Escuadrilla*	1ª/21	CR.32
3/10/38	*Escuadrilla*	1ª/21	CR.32
3/10/38	*Escuadrilla*	1ª/21	CR.32

Date	Name/Unit	Unit	Aircraft
4/10/38	*Escuadrilla?*	*Grupo* Nº 21	He 111
4/10/38	J R González Fdez	6ª/21	Bf 109
4/10/38	*Escuadrilla?*	*Grupo* Nº 21	Bf 109
7/10/38	*Escuadrilla*	3ª/21	Bf 109
7/10/38	*Escuadrilla*	5ª/21	Bf 109
7/10/38	*Escuadrilla*	6ª/21	Bf 109
8/10/38	*Escuadrillas*	3ª/21 & *Grupo* Nº 26	He 111 (damaged)
8/10/38	*Escuadrilla*	4ª/21	CR.32
8/10/38	*Escuadrilla*	5ª/21	3 x CR.32s (one on fire)
9/10/38	*Escuadrilla*	6ª/21	He 51
10/10/38	Missing page		
11/10/38	Missing page		
14/10/38	*Escuadrilla*	*Grupo* Nº 21	3 x CR.32s (one on fire)
14/10/38	*Escuadrilla?*	4ª/21	CR.32 (set on fire)
15/10/38	*Escuadrilla*	1ª/26	SM.79?
15/10/38	*Escuadrilla*	6ª/21	Bf 109
15/10/38	*Escuadrilla*	5ª/21	Bf 109
15/10/38	*Escuadrilla*	3ª/21	CR.32
15/10/38	*Escuadrilla*	3ª/21	2x CR.32s
15/10/38	*Escuadrilla*	3ª/21	CR.32
15/10/38	*Escuadrilla*	4ª/21	3 x CR.32s (two on fire)
15/10/38	*Escuadrilla*	5ª/21	2 x CR.32s (two on fire)
30/10/38	*Escuadra* Nº 11	??	3 x CR.32s (one on fire)
30/10/38	*Escuadrilla*	3ª/21	CR.32 (set on fire)
30/10/38	*Escuadrilla*	4ª/21	CR.32 (set on fire)
31/10/38	F Meroño Pellicer	6ª/21	Bf 109 (half-share)
31/10/38	A García Cano	6ª/21	Bf 109 (half-share)
1/11/38	*Escuadrilla*	6ª/21	2 x CR.32s
1/11/38	J Torn Roca	1ª/26	CR.32
1/11/38	J Bastida Porres	1ª/26	CR.32
1/11/38	L Población Cuenca	1ª/26	CR.32
1/11/38	J Torn Roca	1ª/26	CR.32 (half-share)
1/11/38	A Vallés Gateu	1ª/26	CR.32 (half-share)
1/11/38	J Vela Díaz	1ª/26	CR.32 (half-share)
1/11/38	E Ramírez Bravo	4ª/26	CR.32
1/11/38	J Falcó Sanmartín	3ª/26	CR.32
1/11/38	J Garre Solano	3ª/26	CR.32
1/11/38	A Muñoz López	3ª/26	CR.32
1/11/38	F Sánchez Matos	3ª/26	CR.32
1/11/38	J Santander Menéndez	3ª/26	CR.32
1/11/38	J Tremosa Arnavat	3ª/26	CR.32
1/11/38	E Corbalán Marín	3ª/26	CR.32
1/11/38	J Redondo Martín	1ª/21	CR.32 (half-share)
1/11/38	J A Cano Arnáiz	1ª/21	CR.32 (half-share)
1/11/38	P Dosta Fossá	5ª/21	CR.32 (half-share)
1/11/38	*Escuadrilla*	6ª/21	CR.32
1/11/38	J Santamaría	1ª/21	CR.32 (half-share)
1/11/38	*Escuadrilla*	3ª/21	CR.32 (half-share)
2/11/38	M Fernández Morales	6ª/21	CR.32
2/11/38	J Simón Valverde	1ª/21	CR.32
2/11/38	*Escuadrilla*	1ª/21	Bf 109
2/11/38	*Escuadrilla*	6ª/21	CR.32
3/11/38	P Rueda Hernández	4ª/21	Bf 109
3/11/38	V Llivería Grau	1ª/26	Bf 109
3/11/38	*Escuadrilla*	1ª/26	Twin-engined bomber
3/11/38	*Escuadrilla*	4ª/26	Twin-engined bomber
3/11/38	*Escuadrilla*	3ª/21	Bf 109
3/11/38	P Dosta Fossá	5ª/21	CR.32
3/11/38	J M Bravo Fernández	PM/21	Bf 109
3/11/38	*Escuadrilla*	6ª/21	Do 17 (half-share)
3/11/38	*Escuadrilla*	1ª/21	Do 17 (half-share)
3/11/38	*Escuadrilla*	5ª/21	Do 17 (half-share)
6/11/38	*Escuadra*	Nº 11 ??	Bf 109
8/11/38	*Escuadrilla*	6ª/21	He 51
9/11/38	A Vallés Gateu	1ª/26	CR.32
9/11/38	E Vilatela Soria	1ª/21	CR.32
9/11/38	Santamaría	1ª/21	CR.32
9/11/38	*Escuadrilla*	6ª/21	CR.32
9/11/38	*Escuadrilla*	3ª/21	CR.32
21/12/38	*Escuadrilla*	6ª/21	2 x CR.32s (set on fire)
24/12/38	M Fernández Sánchez	6ª/21	CR.32 (half-share)
24/12/38	González	6ª/21	CR.32 (half-share)
24/12/38	A Morales Escamilla	6ª/21	CR.32 (half-share)
26/12/38	M Fernández Ferreiro	7ª/21	CR.32
26/12/38	P Pérez Gómez	7ª/21	CR.32
26/12/38	P Jiménez Ruiz	7ª/21	CR.32
28/12/38	J Redondo Martín	1ª/21	Bf 109 (half-share)
28/12/38	J Ramoneda Vilardaga	1ª/21	Bf 109 (half-share)
28/12/38	*Escuadra* Nº 11	??	3 x CR.32s
28/12/38	*Escuadra* Nº 11	??	3 x CR.32s (probables)
29/12/38	J M Cano Arnáiz	1ª/21	CR.32 (set on fire)
29/12/38	P Pérez Gómez	7ª/21	Bf 109
29/12/38	*Escuadrilla*	3ª/21	2 x Bf 109s
30/12/38	F Tarazona Torán	3ª/21	Bf 109
30/12/38	*Escuadrilla*	6ª/21	Bf 109
30/12/38	J Lloréns Bonet	3ª/26	CR.32
30/12/38	F Alférez Jiménez	4ª/26	CR.32
30/12/38	N J Fernández Díaz	1ª/21	Bf 109
3/1/39	*Escuadra* Nº 11	??	CR.32 (set on fire)
3/1/39	*Escuadra* Nº 11	??	2 x CR.32s (probable)
5/1/39	*Escuadrilla*	4ª/21	He 111 (half-share)
5/1/39	Escuadrilla	7ª/21	He 111 (half-share)
8/1/39	??	*Grupo* Nº 26	CR.32
9/1/39	*Escuadrilla*	4ª/21	Bf 109 (set on fire)
12/1/39	*Escuadra* Nº 11	??	Do 17 (probable)
19/1/39	A Escardó Soler	4ª/21	Bf 109
19/1/39	*Escuadra* Nº 11	??	Bf 109 (probable)
21/1/39	*Escuadra* Nº 11	??	Bf 109
21/1/39	*Escuadra* Nº 11	??	Ju 87
21/1/39	F Alférez Jiménez	1ª/26	Ju 87
21/1/39	M Castillo Puerta	4ª/26	Bf 109
23/1/39	??	*Grupo* Nº 21	He 111 (probable)

1

Nieuport Ni-H.52 '11-33/3-58' of sargento Andrés García La Calle, the *Grupo* N° 11, Getafe, 28 July 1936

This aircraft crash-landed on the Madrid sierra, where it was profusely photographed and presented by both sides as 'a shot down enemy'. The fighter retained its pre-war all-silver finish, displaying three-colour cockades and rudder striping, together with the black panther badge of the *Grupo* N° 11 on the fin and the group's fuselage code '11'. The numeral '3' in the serial number refers to the aircraft type. The Martinsyde F 4 was designated the Type 1, the Nieuport Ni.29 the Type 2 and the Hawker Spanish Fury the Type 4.

2

Nieuport Ni-H.52 '3-74' of alférez Manuel Aguirre López, the 1ª *Escuadrilla* of the *Grupo* N° 21, Andújar, September 1936

By September 1936 the military *coup* had become a full-scale war, and both sides had established markings to distinguish their military aircraft. The Republicans adopted red bands around the rear fuselage – which covered the group codes – and red wing bands. The *Grupo* N° 21 inherited the aircraft of the *Grupo* N° 11, hence the former's group badge on the fin of '3-74'.

3

Nieuport Ni-H.52 '3-24' of sargento Fernando Romero Tejero, the *Patrulla de caza* of *Escuadrilla* Y-2, Guadix, 28 July 1936

Looking virtually identical to '3-74', this aircraft was force-landed by Romero when its engine failed during a scramble from Guadix.

4

Nieuport Ni-H.52 (serial unknown) of alférez Jesús García Herguido, the *Grupo* N° 23, Sariñena, August to October 1936

The red markings on this unidentified machine were new following the commencement of the civil war, but the four-leafed clover on the fin was the original pre-war badge of the *Grupo* N° 13. Most surviving Republican Nieuports were camouflaged with green paint during 1937.

5

Hawker Spanish Fury '4-1' of alférez Andrés García La Calle, the 2ª *Escuadrilla* of the *Grupo de Caza* N° 11, Alicante, early 1937

La Calle scored several victories while flying this aircraft, which is depicted here as it appeared after being repaired in Alicante in early 1937. The three all-silver Spanish Furies available when war broke out remained with the Republicans, '4-3' later being cannibalised to keep '4-1' airworthy.

6

Hawker Spanish Fury '4-2' of alférez Félix Urtubi Ercilla, the *Grupo de Caza* N° 11, detached to Don Benito, August 1936

Urtubi flew this fighter until he crash-landed it behind enemy lines in August 1936. The Nationalists restored the aeroplane to flying condition in late 1936, although it subsequently crashed once again. The Spanish Fury was eventually returned to airworthiness in 1938.

7

Dewoitine D.372 'White 6' of the *Grupo de Caza* N° 11, Getafe, late September 1936

The Dewoitine parasol fighters arrived in Spain in natural or aluminium finish, over which Republican markings were applied. Peña flew a similar aircraft until he was shot down over the Toledo front on 27 September 1936. A camouflage finish was later applied to the surviving aircraft.

8

Loire 46 'White 3' of alférez García La Calle, the 2ª *Escuadrilla* of the *Grupo de Caza* N° 11, Getafe, summer 1936

The Loire 46 fighters also arrived in natural metal finish, over which Republican markings were applied. The most famous fighter ace of the early war period, La Calle flew a number of missions in these elegant French fighters and made a forced landing in one of them.

9

Dewoitine D.510 'CW-001' of sargento José Sarrió Calatayud, the 1ª *Escuadrilla* of the *Grupo de Defensa de Costas* N° 71, Reus detachment, March 1938

Sarrió was flying this French-built monoplane when he shot down a *Legion Condor* He 59 seaplane during a night engagement on 21 March 1938. The aircraft's wheel spats had probably been removed to avoid the wheels becoming stuck in mud, as only Barajas airfield boasted a tarmac surface during the civil war. The letters 'CW' in the serial number refer to the aircraft type, *Caza Dewoitine*.

10

Boeing Model 281 (serial unknown) of capitán Ramón Puparelli Francia, Alcalá de Henares, October 1936

Originally displaying an olive drab paint scheme, this one-off Boeing demonstrator was requisitioned by the Spanish government and received the normal Republican markings. Puparelli was commander of the Republican fighter force when he was shot down and wounded while flying this machine on 21 October 1936.

11

Polikarpov I-15 'White 57' of teniente Leopoldo Morquillas Rubio, CO of the *Escuadrilla de Caza del Norte*, La Albericia and Penilla de Cayón airfields, Northern front, summer 1937

The gull-winged Polikarpov I-15s were coded in the 'CA-' series, whereas the flattop-winged I-15bis were in the 'CC-' series. On many aircraft (as in this case) only the numeral was applied to the fin or rudder, however. Some fighters, like 'White 57', had black-painted engine cowlings.

12

Polikarpov I-15 'CA-038/White 038' of teniente Juan Comas Borrás, CO of the 3ª _Escuadrilla_ of the _Grupo_ N° 26, Figueras, summer-autumn 1937

The square and rectangle painted onto the fin of this aircraft were two of several geometrical tactical markings – circles and triangles were also applied – used to identify the machine flown by each _escuadrilla_ CO in the group. It is thought that this practice applied only to aircraft assigned to the _Grupo_ N° 26.

13

Polikarpov I-15 'CA-205/White 205' of teniente José Falcó San Martín, CO of the _Patrulla de Vuelo Nocturno_, El Prat de Llobregat, late 1938/early 1939

A photograph of a smiling José Falcó San Martin sitting in this _Chato_ ready for take-off at night was one of the most widely circulated images to emerge from Spain of late-war Republican fighters and their pilots.

14

Polikarpov I-15 'CA-131/White 131' of teniente Antonio Nieto Sandoval-Díaz, CO of the 3ª _Escuadrilla_ of the _Grupo_ N° 26, Monjos, autumn 1938

Nieto Sandoval, who succeeded Zambudio as unit CO, flew this machine in late 1938. The fighter's '3E' code displayed within a white square was used to identify the I-15 flown by the CO of the 3ª _Escuadrilla_ within the group.

15

Polikarpov I-15 'CA-141' of capitán Vicente Castillo Monzó, the _Grupo_ N° 26, Catalonia, late 1938/early 1939

Castillo Monzó, who was the last CO of the _Grupo_ N° 26, adopted Disney's popular 'Mickey Mouse' cartoon character as his personal emblem. Some pilots also wore flying jackets featuring cloth 'Mickey Mouse' badges. The 3.J/88 _Staffel_ of the _Legion Condor_ adopted the same character for its emblem.

16

Polikarpov I-15 'CA-063' of teniente Francisco Viñals Guarro, the 2ª _Escuadrilla_ of the _Grupo_ N° 26, Saceruela, summer 1938

Although the shade of the green uppersurface camouflage that adorned most Republican aircraft is not controversial, Spanish aviation historians cannot agree about the colours applied to the undersurfaces of these aircraft. It is usually depicted as light blue, as seen here, but there is some strong documentary – although not _graphic_ – evidence that it may in fact have been doped aluminium.

17

Polikarpov I-15bis 'White CC-091' of teniente Miguel Castillo Puertas, the 4ª _Escuadrilla_ of the _Grupo_ N° 26, Catalonia, early 1939

Castillo Puertas El Andaluz, not to be confused with Vicente Castillo Monzó 'El Valenciano', succeeded teniente Emilio Ramírez Bravo as CO of the 4ª _Escuadrilla_ in the final stages of the civil war. Castillo Puertas saw plenty of action during the bitter fighting on the Northern front, as well as in other areas of Spain.

18

Polikarpov I-15bis 'CC-083' of teniente Antonio Nieto Sandoval-Díaz, the 3ª _Escuadrilla_ of the _Grupo_ N° 26, Catalonia, March-April 1939

Nieto fled in this _Superchato_ to Carcassonne, in France, after the fall of Catalonia. The letters 'CC' in the serial number refer to the aircraft type.

19

Polikarpov I-16 Type 6 'CM-125' of capitán Manuel Zarauza Clavero, CO of the 4ª _Escuadrilla_ of the _Grupo_ N° 21, Valencia, summer 1938

The 'Popeye' cartoon character displayed on the rudder of this aircraft was the squadron badge of the 4ª _Escuadrilla_. There were many variations on this theme, and in this case the figure is holding a tiny umbrella. The cockpit hood was rarely closed on these aircraft. The Republicans' ranking ace, Zarauza almost certainly used this machine to great effect during the campaigns in Aragon and Levante. Participating in more than 100 aerial battles, he claimed to have shot down 23 enemy aircraft (a number in 'CM-125').

20

Polikarpov I-16 Type 10 'CM-157' of teniente Eduardo Claudín, CO of the 1ª _Escuadrilla_ of the _Grupo_ N° 21, Liria, January 1938

The letters 'CM' in the serial number refer to the aircraft type, _Caza Mosca_. Type 10 I-16s were popularly known as _Supermoscas_, for although the extra weaponry fitted to the aircraft had a somewhat slower rate of fire, the second pair of ShKAS guns offered a heavier punch. Claudín's 1ª _Escuadrilla_ moved to Liria, in Valencia, in late 1937, and on 20 January 1938 he claimed a CR.32 destroyed while flying from here in 'CM-157' – his normal mount at this time. Following Claudín's outstanding leadership of the 1ª _Escuadrilla_ during the hard-fought Teruel campaign he was promoted to capitán in March 1938.

21

Polikarpov I-16 Type 10 'CM-225' of mayor Manuel Zarauza Clavero, the _Grupo_ N° 21 staff, Valencia, autumn 1938

Zarauza replaced his I-16 Type 6 'CM-125' with this red tailed _Supermosca_ during the late summer of 1938. 'CM-225' was another Republican icon of the war in the air over Spain, the fighter's vivid red fin and tailplanes allowing for quick identification of the _grupo_ CO's aircraft during an aerial engagement.

22

Polikarpov I-16 Type 10 'CM-260' of teniente Antonio Arias Arias, CO of the 4ª _Escuadrilla_ of the _Grupo_ N° 21, El Vendrell, autumn 1938

This fighter displays a variation of the 'Popeye' cartoon character on its rudder, this marking adorning most 4ª _Escuadrilla_ machines. Another variation on this theme was 'Popeye' clutching a can of spinach in his hand. Arias flew 'CM-260' throughout the battle of the Ebro, using it to claim his final three civil war victories (all Bf 109s). These successes subsequently led to him being promoted to the rank of capitán in October 1938.

23

Polikarpov I-16 Type 10 'CM-193' of teniente Francisco Tarazona Torán, CO of the 3ª *Escuadrilla* of the *Grupo* Nº 21, Vilajuiga, February 1939

This aircraft was formerly flown by high-scoring ace José María Bravo Fernández. Indeed, the fighter was photographed with Bravo sat beside it being shaved, and later with Tarazona leaning on the tail. These were two of the most widely circulated images of Republican aces to emerge from the civil war. The I-16 displays a double-six domino on its rudder. Tarazona claimed his last success in this machine on 30 December 1938 when he downed a Bf 109. On 7 February 1939 he was lucky to escape with his life when 'CM-193' was attacked by *Legion Condor* aircraft while he was attempting to takeoff from Vilajuiga. Although Tarazona maintained that 'CM-193' was destroyed in the incident, other sources contradict that assertion. Historian Juan Arráez believes

the aircraft was in airworthy condition when it was captured by Nationalist troops, while Thomas Sarbaugh says that contemporary French newspapers reported that *Moscas* 'CM-193', 'CM-244' and 'CM-202' managed to land near Gironde on 5 February 1939.

24

Polikarpov I-16 Type 10 'CM-249' of capitán José María Bravo Fernández of the *Grupo* Nº 21, el Plá de Cabra, summer 1938

'CM-249', which also displays a double-six domino on its rudder, was one of several *Moscas* used by Bravo during his highly successful spell in the frontline in the summer of 1938. The I-16 owned and flown by the *Fundación Infante de Orleáns* museum is painted to represent Bravo's aircraft, and it can be seen flying regularly from Cuatro Vientos air base, Madrid.

BIBLIOGRAPHY

ARCHIVES

Archivo Histórico Militar (Ávila)
Partes diarios de información y operaciones de las Fuerzas Aéreas de la República

Archivo General de la Guerra Civil Española (Salamanca)
Partes de operaciones de la Zona Aérea del Norte y de la 6ª Region Aérea (Santander)
Listas de revista de la 6ª Region Aérea
Diario Oficial de Defensa, 26, 33, 37, 60, 69, 87, 131, 136, 143, 156, 171, 182, 190, 194, 198, 203, 217, 224, 228, 245, 247, 263, 265, 268, 272, 274, 285, 293, 301, 314, 326, 328, 333, unnumbered issue dated 30 July 1937
Diario Oficial de Guerra no 10
D O de la Generalitat no 320
Diario Oficial de Marina y Aire nos 99, 103, 116, 179, 204, 219, 221, 230, 278, 295
Gaceta de Madrid no 254
Gaceta de la República nos 2, 6, 21, 28, 30, 37, 58, 78, 83, 99, 110, 138, 219, 323, 326, 329, 348
Orden Circular no 24.676

Archivo Histórico del Ejército del Aire (Villaviciosa de Odón-Madrid)
Diario de la Escuadra de Caza Nº 11 (incomplete)
Partes de operaciones e informacion de las Fuerzas Aéreas republicanas
Expedientes personales y judiciales de pilotos de caza republicanos

Unpublished Sources
Personal correspondence and interviews with Republican fighter pilots
Juan Comas Borrás's unpublished memoirs

BOOKS

Arias Arias, Antonio, *Arde el cielo*. A Delgado Romero, Silla, 1995
Bravo, José María and De Madariaga, Rafael, *El 'seis doble'*. Fundación AENA, Madrid, 2007
De Milany, Joan, *Un aviador de la República,* Nova Terra, Barcelona, 1971
Lario Sánchez, Juan, *Habla un aviador de la República,* Gregorio del Toro Editor, Madrid, 1973
Permuy López, Rafael A, *Los ases de la República,* Galland Books, Valladolid, 2008
Permuy López, Rafael A, *Los pilotos de caza de la aviación republicana* (volume 1), Quirón Ediciones, Valladolid, 2001
Sainz Cidoncha, Carlos, *Aviación republicana.* (3 volumes), Almena, Madrid, 2006
Salas Larrazábal, Jesús, *Caza rusa en España* (2 volumes), Ministerio de Defensa, Madrid, 2009
Salas Larrazábal, Jesús, *Guerra aérea. 1936-39* (4 volumes), Ministerio de Defensa, Madrid, several years
Salas Larrazábal, Jesús, *La Guerra de España desde el aire,* Ariel, Barcelona, 1969
Sanz Bocos, Miguel Ángel, *Memorias de un chico de Vallecas,* Que vayan ellos, Albacete, 2011
Tarazona Torán, Francisco, *Yo fui piloto de caza rojo,* San Martín, Madrid, 1974

INDEX

References to illustrations are shown in **bold**. Plates are shown with page and caption locators in brackets.